A Guide to Proper Usage of Spoken Chinese

A Guide to Proper Usage of Spoken Chinese

Second Edition

漢·語·口·語·指·引

Tian Shou-he

SMC PUBLISHING INC.
Taipei

ISBN 957-638-347-1

Contents

List of 114 Entries

Acknowledgments

I am grateful to my students and colleagues for calling to my attention many of the difficulties with Chinese usage and for helping me to overcome them. I would also like to acknowledge the great debt I owe to Professor Liu Ming, who first inspired me to take up the study of Chinese linguistics.

Preface

Teachers and students of Chinese have long felt the need for a reference book to accompany Chinese textbooks at the elementary and intermediate levels. As China opens its doors to the world, and as more people begin to study the Chinese language in order to communicate with the Chinese people, the need for a book such as this one is even greater. From the student's point of view, a reference book must meet recurring needs in three areas:

1. Interlingual area: how to recognize and deal with interference from the student's native language (English);
2. Grammar: how to differentiate between two grammatically similar points;
3. Vocabulary: how to distinguish between two semantically similar points.

As far as the teacher is concerned, a reference book should serve as a means of easy and efficient consultation for the essential grammatical and vocabulary points given in beginning Chinese textbooks.

This book aims to address the needs of both teacher and student, and, in particular, to remedy a situation in which beginners of Chinese, owing to the dearth of reference books, inadvertently learn some incorrect grammatical and vocabulary points which subsequently become "fossilized". Ultimately the difficulty lies not so much in understanding correctly from the start, as in "unlearning" any points which may have originally been learned incorrectly. Thus the importance of getting things straight from the start cannot be overemphasized.

As a result of over ten years of teaching and observation, I have identified and included in this book over 200 points of grammar and vocabulary which frequently cause trouble to students of Chinese. A comparative approach has been adopted to deal with these points. Comparisons are made:

1. between Chinese and English;
2. between two grammatical points;
3. between two vocabulary points.

Moreover, primary meanings with examples, or a brief explanation of the problem with examples, or both, are provided for each entry. Typical errors (mostly original) are supplied whenever they are useful by way of explanation. Reinforcement exercises with key are given at the back. A Pinyin/English index has been carefully prepared with the hope of facilitating the use of this book thereby making it a more helpful reference tool.

Tian Shou-he
Hong Kong

How to Use the Book

A list of 104 entries comprising more than 200 difficult points of grammar and vocabulary is given in this book. The entries are arranged alphabetically and are numbered. The best way to find a point is to look in the index at the back. Most grammatical explanations and problems are indexed under several different references. For instance, if you want to find out the functions of *le* and the distinction between *le* and past events with *shi . . . de* construction, you can look in the index under "completed action", "*le*", "*shi . . . de* construction" or "past events".

1. 吧 ba and 嗎 ma

The sentence-final particle "吧 ba" has two primary functions:
(1) It is used as a modal particle tagged to commands, suggestions, requests, etc.

1.1 快 點兒 吃 吧。
Kuài diǎnr chī ba.
Eat a little faster, will you?

1.2 讓 我 幫 你 拿 吧。
Ràng wǒ bāng nǐ ná ba.
Let me take it for you.

(2) It is used at the end of a sentence to ask for agreement or confirmation. English sentences with question tags — e.g. "You are a student, aren't you?" — when translated into Chinese normally call for the use of "吧 ba".

1.3 他 姓 張 吧？
Tā xìng Zhāng ba?
His last name is Zhang, isn't it?

1.4 你 很 想 她 吧？
Nǐ hěn xiǎng tā ba?
You miss her a lot, don't you?

"吧 ba" and "嗎 ma" compared:

The basic difference between "吧 ba" and "嗎 ma" as question particles is that "嗎 ma" is used for questions that seek information or for rhetorical questions, while "吧 ba" is used for questions that seek confirmation or agreement.

1.5 他 回國了 嗎？
Tā huíguóle ma?
Has he returned to his own country?

1.6 他 回國了 吧？
Tā huíguóle ba?
He's returned to his own country, hasn't he?

2. 把 bǎ

Typical errors:

I ate a piece of candy.
我 把 一 塊 糖 吃了。
Wǒ bǎ yí kuài táng chīle.

Please read the book over.
請 把 書 看。
Qǐng bǎ shū kàn.

Correct usage:

我 把 糖 吃了。
Wǒ bǎ táng chīle.

請 把 書 看看。
Qǐng bǎ shū kànkan.

The "ba" construction changes the usual Chinese sentence pattern "Subject + Verb + Object" (S V O) by transferrring the object to a pre-verbal position. Thus the new pattern is "Subject + Ba + Object + Verb" (S Ba O V). We use the "ba" construction because when the object is moved to a pre-verbal position we can readily and quickly proceed from given information (the object) to new information (the verbal phrase), which is the focus of the sentence. Note the following points:
(1) The object in a "ba" construction is specific rather than generic. The listener knows what object the speaker refers to, either because he/she has some prior knowledge of it, or the speaker has just qualified it. Hence the sentence "我把一塊糖 (unspecific) 吃了" is incorrect.
(2) When we use the "ba" construction the main verb of the sentence should not be exposed at the end of the sentence. It can be complemented in several ways by:

(a) *Using the verb suffix "了"*:

2.1 他 把 車 賣了。
Tā bǎ chē màile.
He sold his car.

(b) *Using an indirect object*:

2.2 把 錢 給 他。
Bǎ qián gěi tā.
Give him the money.

(c) *Reduplicating the verb*:

2.3 別 忘了 把 書 看看。
Bié wàngle bǎ shū kànkan.
Don't forget to read the book.

(d) *Using number + measure*:

2.4 把 西瓜 切成 四 塊。
Bǎ xīguā qiēchéng sì kuài.
Cut the watermelon into four slices.

(e) *Using directional or place words*:

2.5 請 把 菜 拿來。
Qǐng bǎ cài nálai.
Bring the dishes over, please.

2.6 他 一定 要 把 照相機 放在 箱子 裏頭。
Tā yídìng yào bǎ zhàoxiàngjī fàngzai xiāngzi lǐtou.
He insisted on having the camera placed in the suitcase.

(f) *Using descriptive complement*:

Ba + Object + Verb + de Complement
Ba + Object + Adjective + de Complement

2.7 昨天 把 我 吃得 站不起來 了。
Zuótian bǎ wǒ chīde zhànbuqǐlái le.
I ate so much yesterday that I couldn't stand up.

2.8 他 把 我 氣得 睡不着 覺。
Tā bǎ wǒ qìde shuìbuzháo jiào.
He made me so mad that I couldn't sleep.

3. 半 bàn, 一半 yí bàn, 一個半 yí ge bàn

Typical errors:

When foreign students wish to say "half an hour", they often say,

半鐘頭　bàn zhōngtóu
一半鐘頭　yí bàn zhōngtóu
一個半鐘頭　yí ge bàn zhōngtóu
一半個鐘頭　yí bàn ge zhōngtóu

Correct usage:

半　個　鐘頭
bàn　ge　zhōngtóu

半 bàn

When we want to say "half of something" in Chinese, we use "半 bàn" *followed* by a measure word and a noun.

3.1　我　要　吃　半　個　蛋糕。
Wǒ　yào　chī　bàn　ge　dàngāo.
I want to have half of the cake.

3.2　半　個　鐘頭　不　夠。
Bàn　ge　zhōngtóu　bú　gòu.
Half an hour is not enough.

When "半 bàn" is *preceded* by a number and a measure word, it means the whole number plus a half.

3.3　一　斤　半　米　不　夠　吃。
Yì　jīn　bàn　mǐ　bú　gòu　chī.
One and a half catties of rice are not enough.

3.4　英文報　賣　三　塊　半。
Yīngwénbào　mài　sān　kuài　bàn.
The English paper costs three dollars and fifty cents.

一半 yí bàn

"一半 yí bàn" also means "half", it is normally used after a noun or a verb.

3.5 鷄的 一 半 太 生， 一 半 太 熟。
Jī de yí bàn tài shēng, yí bàn tài shóu.
One half of the chicken is too raw while the other half is overcooked.

3.6 這 件 事 我們 已經 商量了 一 半 了。
Zhèi jiàn shì wǒmen yǐjing shāngliangle yí bàn le.
We have already discussed this matter halfway through.

3.7 他 吃飯 吃了 一 半 就 走了。
Tā chīfàn chīle yí bàn jiù zǒule.
He left halfway through his meal.

"半 bàn" and "一半 yí bàn" compared:

(1) Although "半 bàn" and "一半 yíbàn" both mean "half", when they are used to modify a noun, "一半 yí bàn" generally refers to "half of a specific thing" while "半 bàn" refers to "half of anything".
(2) We may use "一半 yí bàn" to modify a verb, but we may not do so with "半 bàn".
(3) "一半 yí bàn" can stand alone as a short answer while "半 bàn" has to have a measure word after it. For example, when offered a glass of Maotai one can either say, "一半 yí bàn" (half) or "半杯 bàn bēi" (half a glass).

3.8 故事 的 前 一 半 没有 意思。
Gùshi de qián yí bàn méiyou yìsi.
The first half of the story is uninteresting.

3.9 他 就 講了 半 個 故事。
Tā jiù jiǎngle bàn ge gùshi.
He only told half a story.

一個半 yí ge bàn

"一個半 yí ge bàn" simply means "one and a half".

3.10 一 個 半 鐘頭
Yí ge bàn zhōngtóu
One and a half hours

3.11 一 張 半 紙
Yì zhāng bàn zhǐ
One and a half sheets of paper

4. 幫 bāng and 幫忙 bāngmáng

Typical errors:

I help him.
我 幫忙 他。
Wǒ bāngmáng tā.

I help him carry the luggage.
我 幫忙 他 拿 行李。
Wǒ bāngmáng tā ná xíngli.

Correct usage:

我 幫 他 忙。
Wǒ bāng tā máng.

我 幫 他 拿 行李。
Wǒ bāng tā ná xíngli.

"幫 bāng" is used for situations such as "He helped me to do such and such a thing". The usual pattern is "Noun_1 Bāng Noun_2 + Verb".

4.1 他 幫 我 看 孩子。
Tā bāng wǒ kān háizi.
He helps me to baby-sit the children.

4.2 請 你 幫 小 李 解決 這 個 問題。
Qǐng nǐ bāng xiǎo Lǐ jiějué zhèi ge wèntí.
Please help little Li to solve this problem.

"幫忙 bāngmáng" is used in two ways:

(1) It can take a personal pronoun. When it does, the personal pronoun is inserted between "幫 bāng" and "忙 máng". This usage is only for general help without specifying what the matter is. Usually few words are used to qualify "忙 máng".

4.3 請 你 幫 我 一 個 忙， 可以 嗎？
Qǐng nǐ bāng wǒ yí ge máng, kěyǐ ma?
Can you do me a favor?

4.4 老 張 幫了 我們 很 多 忙。
Lǎo Zhāng bāngle wǒmen hěn duō máng.
Old Zhang helped us a lot.

4.5 她 幫了 我 一 個 大 忙。
Tā bāngle wǒ yí ge dà máng.
She has done me a great favor.

4.6 他 幫了 我 一 個 倒忙。
Tā bāngle wǒ yí ge dàománg.
Instead of helping me, he caused me some trouble.

Note: "倒忙 dàománg" literally means "upside down help". In other words, help is turned into trouble.

(2) It is used to indicate a specific help and is usually followed by a verb phrase. Note that in this usage we cannot use a pronoun after it.

4.7 請 你 幫忙 打 一 封 信，好 嗎？
Qǐng nǐ bāngmáng dǎ yì fēng xìn, hǎo ma?
Can you help type a letter?

4.8 你 來 幫忙 包 餃子 嗎？
Nǐ lái bāngmáng bāo jiǎozi ma?
Did you come to help make dumplings?

5. 倍 bèi

"倍 bèi" means "fold" or "times". It follows three patterns:

(1) $Noun_1$ shì $Noun_2$ de Number-Bèi
(2) $Noun_1$ yǒu $Noun_2$ de Number-Bèi
(3) $Noun_1$ bǐ $Noun_2$ Adjective Number-Bèi

When translated into English, the "Number + Bèi" in the first two patterns corresponds with "Number + Times" in English. The third pattern is quite different. For example, if "A bǐ B duō liǎng bèi", the English equivalent would be "A is three times that of B". The logic for a two-fold comparison (as in Chinese) rather than a three-fold one (as in English) can be readily seen in the following diagram:

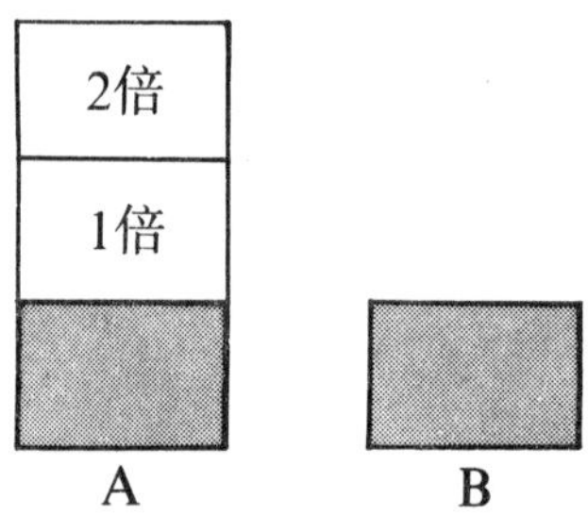

A has two more parts than B does; therefore "A bǐ B duō liǎng bèi", *not* "sān bèi".

5.1 他 的 車速 是 我 的 兩 倍。
Tā de chēsù shì wǒ de liǎng bèi.
His driving speed is twice that of mine.

5.2 他 的 車速 有 我 的 兩 倍。
Tā de chēsù yǒu wǒ de liǎng bèi.
His driving speed is twice that of mine.

5.3 他 開車 開得 比 我 快 一 倍。
Tā kāichē kāide bǐ wǒ kuài yí bèi.
He drives twice as fast as I do.

6. 比 bǐ

Typical errors:

I'm much taller than he.
我　比 他　很　高。
Wǒ　bǐ　tā　hěn　gāo.

我　比 他　高　極了。
Wǒ　bǐ　tā　gāo　jíle.

Correct usage:

我　比 他　高　多了/　得　多。
Wǒ　bǐ　tā　gāo　duōle/　de　duō.

"比 bǐ" means "compare to", and is used in comparisons. If we want to say "A is older than B", the Chinese equivalent would be "A bǐ B dà". As in English, when comparing two things, we do not use "很 hěn" (very) in a comparison nor do we use adverbs of degree such as "極了 jíle" (extremely), "太 tài" (too), "真 zhēn" (really), etc.

6.1 他　比 我　能　吃苦。
Tā　bǐ　wǒ　néng　chīkǔ.
He is more able to suffer than I.

6.2 她　比 他　大　一點兒。
Tā　bǐ　tā　dà　yìdiǎnr.
She is a little older than he.

6.3 這　部　電腦　比 那　部　貴　得多/　多了。
Zhèi　bù　diànnǎo　bǐ　nèi　bù　guì　deduō/　duōle.
This computer is much more expensive than that one.

6.4 這　個　電影　比　那　個　好看　得多。
Zhèi　ge　diànyǐng　bǐ　nèi　ge　hǎokàn　deduō.
This movie is much better than that one.

6.5 這　個　照相機　比　那　個　便宜　一百　塊　錢。
Zhèi　ge　zhàoxiàngjī　bǐ　nèi　ge　piányi　yìbǎi　kuài　qián.
This camera costs one hundred dollars less than that one.

7. 畢業 bìyè

Typical errors:

It's been three years since he graduated from the university.
他 畢業 大學 三 年 了。
Tā bìyè dàxué sān nián le.

他 從 大學 畢業 三 年 了。
Tā cóng dàxué bìyè sān nián le.

Correct usage:

他 大學 畢業 三 年 了。
Tā dàxué bìyè sān nián le.

"畢業 bìyè" means "to graduate". It does not take an object nor does it normally need a preposition such as "從 cóng" (from). "A graduate" is "畢業生 bìyèshēng" and "graduate school" is "研究院 yánjiūyuàn".

7.1 他 是 哪 年 大學 畢業 的？
Tā shì něi nián dàxué bìyè de?
What year did he graduate from the university?

7.2 他 大學 畢業 三 年 了。
Tā dàxué bìyè sān nián le.
It's been three years since he graduated from the university.

8. 別客氣 bié kèqi

When we say "別客氣 bié kèqi", we do not mean "Don't be polite; be rude". We use it in three ways:

(1) To one's guest, it means "don't stand on ceremony" or "make yourself at home".

8.1 別 客氣， 請 自己 來。
Bié kèqi, qǐng zìjǐ lái.
Make yourself at home. Please help yourself.

(2) To one's host, it means "don't bother".

8.2 別 客氣， 我 剛 喝過 茶 了。
Bié kèqi, wǒ gāng hēguo chá le.
Don't bother. I've just had some tea.

(3) When responding to other people's thanks, it means "don't mention it".

8.3 **A:** 謝謝 你 的 照片。
Xièxie nǐ de zhàopiàn.
Thank you for your photos.

B: 別 客氣。
Bié kèqi.
Don't mention it.

9. 別的 biéde and 另外 lìngwài

Typical errors:

The other day I met a friend.
別的 天 我 碰見 一 個 朋友。
Biéde tiān wǒ pèngjian yí ge péngyou.

The other friend didn't come.
別的 一 個 朋友 沒 來。
Biéde yí ge péngyou méi lái.

Correct usage:

前 幾 天 我 碰見 一 個 朋友。
Qián jǐ tiān wǒ pèngjian yí ge péngyou.

另外 一 個 朋友 沒 來。
Lìngwài yí ge péngyou méi lái.

"別的 biéde" means "other", "others", "the other" or "the others". Its precise meaning is normally determined by the context. It is only used for plural nouns and is not followed by a quantified noun. In other words, it cannot be followed by a number plus a measure word.

9.1 別的 人 怎麼 想，我 不 管。
Biéde rén zěnme xiǎng, wǒ bù guǎn.
I don't care what others think.

9.2 別的 唱片，我 今天 不 聽了。
Biéde chàngpiàn, wǒ jīntian bù tīngle.
I'm not going to listen to the other records today.

9.3 談 別的 吧。
Tán biéde ba.
Let's change the subject. / Let's talk about other things.

9.4 請 你 告訴 別的 人 我 會 晚 來。
Qǐng nǐ gàosu biéde rén wǒ huì wǎn lái.
Please tell the others that I'll be late.

Note: "The other day" in Chinese is not "別的天 biéde tiān". The correct rendering is "幾天前 jǐ tiān qián" or "前幾天 qián jǐ tiān".

"另外 lìngwài" means "the other" or "other" when it is followed by "的 de + Noun", in which case it is equivalent to "別的 + Noun". We can also use "另外 lìngwài" before "Number + Measure + Noun" or as an adverb before a verb. When it precedes a verb, it conveys the meaning of "in addition" or "one more".

9.5 另外 的 人 走路 去。
Lìngwài de rén zǒulù qù.
The other people will go on foot.

9.6 他 另外 給了 我 五百 塊 錢。
Tā lìngwài gěile wǒ wǔbǎi kuài qián.
He gave me another five hundred dollars.

9.7 爸爸 把 另外 一 輛 車 也 賣了。
Bàba bǎ lìngwài yí liàng chē yě màile.
Father also sold the other car.

9.8 我 另外 叫了 一 個 清湯。
Wǒ lìngwài jiàole yí ge qīngtāng.
In addition, I ordered a clear soup.

To summarize, "別的 biéde" and "另外 lìngwài" are compared below in a diagram:

A 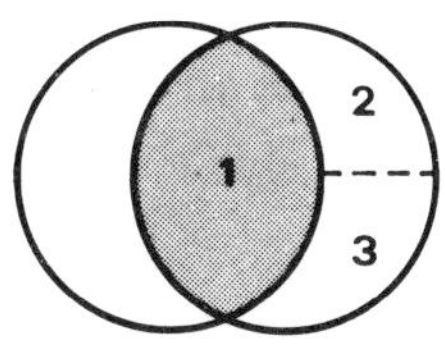 B

A＝別的, B＝另外的

1＝ 別的 / 另外的 } + Plural Noun { generic (other) / specific (the other)

2＝另外 + Verb + Number + Measure + Noun (generic)

3＝Verb + 另外 + Number + Measure + Noun { generic (another, other) / specific (the other)

Note: Whether the noun is generic or specific depends on the context.

10. 不 bù and 別 bié

Typical errors:

He doesn't like to picnic.
他 別 喜歡 野餐。
Tā bié xǐhuan yěcān.

Don't buy it!
不 買！
Bù mǎi!

Correct usage:

他 不 喜歡 野餐。
Tā bù xǐhuan yěcān.

別 買!
Bié mǎi!

When we use negative sentences we normally use "不 bù" followed by a verb, an adjective or an adverb. "不 bù" can also be used as a negative answer to contradict a question.

10.1 他 不 知道 這 件 事。
Tā bù zhīdào zhèi jiàn shì.
He doesn't know about this matter.

10.2 我 一點兒 也 不 着急。
Wǒ yìdiǎnr yě bù zhāojí.
I'm not a bit worried.

10.3 **A:** 他 會 說 普通話 嗎?
Tā huì shuō Pǔtōnghuà ma?
Can he speak Mandarin?

B: 不，他 不 會。
Bù, tā bú huì.
No, he can't.

10.4 **A:** 你 是 老師 吧?
Nǐ shì lǎoshī ba?
I suppose you are a teacher?

B: 不，我 是 做 買賣 的。
Bù, wǒ shì zuò mǎimai de.
No, I'm a businessman.

"别 bié" is generally used for negative imperative sentences. It is equivalent to "不要 búyào".

10.5 别 忘了!
Bié wàngle!
Don't forget it!

10.6 別 動!
Bié dòng!
Don't touch it! / Don't move!

10.7 別 掛上 電話。
Bié guàshang diànhuà.
Don't hang up.

10.8 別 笑 我。
Bié xiào wǒ.
Don't laugh at me.

11. 不想 bù xiǎng and 不覺得 bù juéde

Typical errors:

Don't you think this is very simple?
你 不 想 這 個 很 簡單 嗎？
Nǐ bù xiǎng zhèi ge hěn jiǎndān ma?

I don't think he can do it well.
我 不 想 他 做得好。
Wǒ bù xiǎng tā zuòdehǎo.

Correct usage:

你 不 覺得 這 個 很 簡單 嗎？
Nǐ bù juéde zhè ge hěn jiǎndān ma?

我 想 他 做 不 好。
Wǒ xiǎng tā zuò bù hǎo.

"不想 bù xiǎng" means "do not want to", "do not feel like" or "do not miss" (a person, a pet or a place). It cannot be used for such English expressions as "I don't think..." or "Don't you think ...?" The Chinese equivalents are "我想……不 + Verb" and "你不覺得……嗎?" or "你不認爲……嗎？" (more formal).

11.1 我 今天 不 想 學習。
Wǒ jīntian bù xiǎng xuéxí.
I don't feel like studying today.

11.2 你 想不想 家？
Nǐ xiǎngbuxiǎng jiā?
Do you feel homesick?

11.3 他 想 你 嗎？
Tā xiǎng nǐ ma?
Does he miss you?

11.4 你 不 覺得 他 孩子 可愛 嗎？
Nǐ bù juéde tā háizi kěài ma?
Don't you feel his child is lovable?

11.5 我 想 她 不 會 喜歡 去。
Wǒ xiǎng tā bú huì xǐhuan qù.
I don't think she would like to go.

Since "做不好 zuòbuhǎo" is a resultative verb, the negative form is "Verb + bu + Result".

12. 才 cái

"才 cái" has four primary roles:

(1) It means "only" when it is followed by:
   (a) "Verb + Number + Measure + (Noun)"
   (b) "Number + Measure + (Noun)"

12.1 我 才 有 一 本 字典。
Wǒ cái yǒu yì běn zìdiǎn.
I've only one dictionary.

12.2 他 才 打了 三 場 網球。
Tā cái dǎle sān chǎng wǎngqiú.
He's played only three games of tennis.

12.3 才 星期三，我 等不及 了。
Cái Xīngqīsān, wǒ děngbují le.
It's Wednesday. I can't wait.

12.4 一共 才 五 個 蘋果，不 夠 吃。
Yígòng cái wǔ ge píngguǒ, bú gòu chī.
Altogether, there are only five apples. It's not enough.

(2) It means "just" or "a moment ago" when it is followed by a verb or by another clause with "就 jiù".

12.5 我 才 下班。
Wǒ cái xiàbān.
I just got off from work.

12.6 我們 才 說到 你，你 就 來了。
Wǒmen cái shuōdao nǐ, nǐ jiù láile.
We were just talking about you, and here you are.

(3) It can also mean "only then, not until". We use it to show an action which occurs later than expected.

12.7 他 明天 才 到 北京 去。
Tā míngtian cái dào Běijīng qù.
He's not leaving for Beijing until tomorrow.

12.8 你 怎麼 現在 才 來？
Nǐ zěnme xiànzài cái lái?
How come you only just arrived?

(4) It is used as a modal particle for emphasis. It is somewhat equivalent to English expressions with reinforcement tags such as, "I'm not going to tell him, not I."

12.9 我 才 不 去 告訴 他 呢。
Wǒ cái bú qù gàosu tā ne.
I'm not going to tell him, not I.

12.10 你 才 是 壞蛋 呢。
Nǐ cái shì huàidàn ne.
You're a rotten egg (i.e. bad guy), you are.

Note: In this usage "才 cái" normally takes the modal particle "呢 ne" with it. The pattern is "才……呢 cái ... ne".

13. 長 cháng and 久 jiǔ

Typical error:

This river is very long.
這 條 河 很 久。
Zhèi tiáo hé hěn jiǔ.

Correct usage:

這 條 河 很 長。
Zhèi tiáo hé hěn cháng.

"長 cháng" means "long". We can use it to describe either length or time.

13.1 他 學 中文 的 時間 不 太 長。
Tā xué Zhōngwén de shíjiān bú tài cháng.
He hasn't been studying Chinese for very long.

13.2 長城 真 偉大。
Chángchéng zhēn wěidà.
The Great Wall (lit. long wall) is truly great.

13.3 我 要 講 一 個 長的 故事。
Wǒ yào jiǎng yí ge chángde gùshi.
I'm going to tell (you) a long story.

"久 jiǔ" also means "long". However, it is only used to describe time.

13.4 很 久 沒 見。
Hěn jiǔ méi jiàn.
Long time no see.

13.5 你 在 這兒 住了 多 久 了／多 長 時間 了？
Nǐ zài zhèr zhùle duō jiǔ le/duō cháng shíjiān le?
How long have you been living here?

13.6 很 久 很 久 以前，有 一 位 美麗的 公主。
Hěn jiǔ, hěn jiǔ yǐqián, yǒu yí wèi měilìde gōngzhǔ.
Long, long ago, there lived a beautiful princess.

14. 吃得了 chīdeliǎo, 吃得完 chīdewán, 吃得下 chīdexià, etc.

Typical errors:

Can you get Japanese food in Beijing?
在　北京　會　吃　日本　菜　嗎？
Zài Běijīng huì chī Rìběn cài ma?

在　北京　可以　吃　日本　菜　嗎？
Zài Běijīng kěyǐ chī Rìběn cài ma?

Correct usage:

在　北京　吃得到　(着)　日本　菜　嗎？
Zài Běijīng chīdedào (zháo) Rìběn cài ma?

吃得了 **chīdeliǎo**

"吃得了 chīdeliǎo" is a resultative verb compound. It means "able to eat" (a certain quantity of food). The resultative verb complement "了 liǎo" means the ability or possibility of doing something.

14.1 這麼　多　菜，我們　怎麼　吃得了？
Zhème duō cài, wǒmen zěnme chīdeliǎo?
With so many dishes, how can we finish them?

14.2 你　吃得了　三　碗　飯　嗎？
Nǐ chīdeliǎo sān wǎn fàn ma?
Can you eat three bowls of rice?

吃得完 **chīdewán**

"吃得完 chīdewán" is also a resultative verb. It means "able to finish eating".

14.3 你　五　分　鐘　吃得完　嗎？
Nǐ wǔ fēn zhōng chīdewán ma?
Can you finish eating in five minutes?

14.4 你　今天　吃不完，明天　把　它　吃完。
Nǐ jīntian chībuwán, míngtian bǎ tā chīwán.
If you can't eat it all today, finish it tomorrow.

"吃得了 chīdeliǎo" and "吃得完 chīdewán" compared:

Although "吃得了 chīdeliǎo" and "吃得完 chīdewán" are similar expressions, the following two points should be noted:

(1) "吃得了 chīdeliǎo" is only used in the potential form. The actual form, that is, "吃了了 chīliǎo le" (finished eating) or "没吃了 méi chīliǎo" (did not finish eating) are not acceptable. "吃得完 chīdewán" is used in both potential and actual forms. For example, "他吃完了飯就回家" (He'll go home when he finishes his meal.).

(2) "吃得完 chīdewán" is more explicit with the idea of "finish" than "吃得了 chīdeliǎo". For example, "他吃得了三碗飯，可是五分鐘一定吃不完" (Although he can eat three bowls of rice, he certainly will not be able to finish in five minutes.).

吃得好 **chīdehǎo**

The resultative verb complement "好 hǎo" indicates satisfactory completion. Hence, "吃得好 chīdehǎo" means "can eat satisfactorily or well".

14.5 坐 飛機 我 老 吃不好。
Zuò fēijī wǒ lǎo chībuhǎo.
I never eat well on a plane. (Due to poor food, air sickness, etc.)

14.6 在 他 家裏 吃飯， 誰 也 吃不好。
Zài tā jiāli chīfàn, shéi yě chībuhǎo.
Nobody eats well at his place. (e.g. He never prepares enough food.)

吃得着 **chīdezháo** or 吃得到 **chīdedào**

When we want to know the availability of food in a locality we use "吃得着 chīdezháo" or "吃得到 chīdedào".

14.7 在 北京 吃得到 漢堡包 嗎？
Zài Běijīng chīdedào hànbǎobāo ma?
Can you get hamburger in Beijing?

14.8 在 那 個 飯館 吃得到 "北京 烤鴨" 嗎？
Zài nèi ge fànguǎn chīdedào "Běijīng kǎoyā" ma?
Can you get "Beijing Duck" in that restaurant?

吃得起 **chīdeqǐ**

We use "吃得起 chīdeqǐ" when we want to say "able to afford some food".

14.9 五百 塊 錢 一 桌， 你 吃得起 嗎？
Wǔbǎi kuài qián yì zhuō, nǐ chīdeqǐ ma?
Can you afford a five-hundred-dollar banquet?

14.10 你 吃得起 “魚翅” 嗎？
Nǐ chīdeqǐ “yúchì” ma?
Can you afford to eat “shark's fin”?

吃得下 chīdexià

“吃得下 chīdexià” means “able to eat”. It differs from “吃得了 chīdeliǎo” in that “吃得了 chīdeliǎo” normally refers to one's capacity for eating while “吃得下 chīdexià” refers not only to the same capacity but also to one's appetite, which can be affected by many things. For example, if one's appetite is affected by hot weather conditions then one could say “今天這麼熱，我吃不下飯” (Today it's so hot that I can't eat.). One cannot use “吃不了 chībuliǎo” in this situation.

14.11 我 吃得下 三 碗 飯。
Wǒ chīdexià sān wǎn fàn.
I can eat three bowls of rice.

14.12 我 吃得了 三 碗 飯。
Wǒ chīdeliǎo sān wǎn fàn.
I can eat three bowls of rice.

Both 〈14.11〉 and 〈14.12〉 are acceptable.

14.13 我 不 舒服， 所以 吃不下 飯。
Wǒ bù shūfu, suǒyǐ chībuxià fàn.
I'm not well so I can't eat.

14.14 他 把 我 氣得 吃不下 飯。
Tā bǎ wǒ qìde chībuxià fàn.
He made me so mad that I couldn't eat.

Note: “吃不了 chībuliǎo” is not acceptable in either 〈14.13〉 or 〈14.14〉.

吃得來 chīdelái

We use “吃得來 chīdelái” when we can eat some food which is new to us or which has a particular taste to it.

14.15 你 吃得來 “海參” 嗎？
Nǐ chīdelái “hǎishēn” ma?
Can you eat “sea-cucumber”?

14.16 很多 中國人 都 吃不來 “吉司”。
Hěnduō Zhōngguórén dōu chībulái “jìsi”.
Many Chinese can't take the taste of cheese.

15. 出事 chūshì and 意外 yìwài

Typical error:

He had an accident.
他 有了 一 件 出事。
Tā yǒule yí jiàn chūshì.

Correct usage:

他 出事 了。
Tā chūshì le.

"出事 chūshì" means "to have an accident". It is normally used as a verb (i.e Verb-object Compound). Therefore "He had an accident" should be rendered "他出事了". Since "出事 chūshì" is a verb, the possessive verb "有 yǒu" cannot be used before it.

15.1 他 昨天 開車 出事了。
Tā zuótian kāichē chūshìle.
He had a car accident yesterday.

15.2 她 是 個 容易 出事 的 人。
Tā shì ge róngyi chūshì de rén.
She's accident-prone.

"意外 yìwài" or "事故 shìgù" is used as a noun and it means "accident". The verb we normally use for "意外 yìwài" is "發生 fāshēng", which means "occur".

15.3 意外 是 會 發生 的。
Yìwài shì huì fāshēng de.
Accidents can occur.

15.4 航天 飛機 不幸 發生了 意外。
Hángtiān fēijī búxìng fāshēngle yìwài.
The space shuttle unfortunately had an accident.

16. 從來沒(不) cónglái méi (bù) and 一直沒(不) yìzhí méi (bù)

Typical error:

I never eat fish.
我 一直 不 吃 魚。
Wǒ yìzhí bù chī yú.

Correct usage:

我 從來 不 吃 魚。
Wǒ cónglái bù chī yú.

" 從來沒(不) cónglái méi (bù)" and " 一直沒(不) yìzhí méi (bù)" are both rendered "never" in English. We use " 從來沒 cónglái méi" in the sense of "at no time in the past" and " 一直沒 yìzhí méi" "at no time in a given period of time".

16.1 他 從來 不 撒謊／說謊。
Tā cónglái bù sāhuǎng / shuōhuǎng.
She never lies.

16.2 他 從來 沒 丟過 東西。
Tā cónglái méi diūguo dōngxi.
He has never lost anything before.

16.3 到了 中國 以後，我 一直 沒 見過 他。
Dàole Zhōngguó yǐhòu, wǒ yìzhí méi jiànguo tā.
I have never seen him since I came to China.

16.4 我 昨天 等了 她 一 天，可是 她 一直 都 沒 來。
Wǒ zuótian děngle tā yì tiān, kěshi tā yìzhí dōu méi lái.
Yesterday I waited for her the whole day, but she never showed up.

17. 大家 dàjiā and 每個人 měi ge rén

Typical errors:

Everybody in the world loves peace.
世界　上　大家　都　愛　和平。
Shìjiè shang dàjiā dōu ài hépíng.

Good morning everybody!
每　個　人　早！
Měi ge rén zǎo!

Correct usage:

世界　上　每　個　人　都　愛　和平。
Shìjiè shang měi ge rén dōu ài hépíng.

大家　早！
Dàjiā zǎo!

"大家 dàjiā" means "everybody" in a particular group of people. Note these four points:

(1) It is used when we are stressing the idea of a whole group.
(2) It is used as a definite pronoun.
(3) Personal plural pronouns "我們 wǒmen", "你們 nǐmen" and "他們 tāmen" can be used before "大家 dàjiā".
(4) "大伙兒 dàhuǒr" and "大家伙兒 dàjiāhuǒr" are two colloquial equivalents to "大家 dàjiā".

17.1 我們　大家　都　早睡　早起。
Wǒmen dàjiā dōu zǎoshuì zǎoqǐ.
Everyone of us goes to sleep early and gets up early.

17.2 請　大家　安靜。
Qǐng dàjiā ānjìng.
Please be quiet everybody.

17.3 謝謝　你們　大家　的　好意。
Xièxie nǐmen dàjiā de hǎoyì.
Thank you all for your kindness.

"每個人 měi ge rén" also means "everybody". Note these three points:

(1) We can use it as an indefinite pronoun stressing a whole group.

(2) We can also use it to stress each member of a group.

(3) It can be used after plural pronouns.

17.4 他 想 每 個 人 都 對 他 撒謊/說謊。
Tā xiǎng měi ge rén dōu duì tā sāhuǎng/shuōhuǎng.
He thinks that everybody lies to him.

17.5 每 個 人 都 有 自己 的 問題。
Měi ge rén dōu yǒu zìjǐ de wèntí.
Everybody has their own problems.

17.6 他們 每 個 人 給了 我 十 塊 錢。
Tāmen měi ge rén gěile wǒ shí kuài qián.
Each of them gave me ten dollars.

18. 帶 dài and 拿 ná

We use "帶 dài" to mean "bring or take something/someone with you".

18.1 別 忘了 帶 傘。
Bié wàngle dài sǎn.
Don't forget to take your umbrella with you.

18.2 你 帶 錢 了 嗎？
Nǐ dài qián le ma?
Do you have money with you?

18.3 請 帶 你 孩子 一塊兒 來。
Qǐng dài nǐ háizi yíkuàir lái.
Please bring your children along.

18.4 別 帶着 現金。
Bié dàizhe xiànjīn.
Don't carry cash with you.

We use "拿 ná" to mean "bring or take something to someone/somewhere". It can also mean "to hold".

18.5 請 把 這 些 東西 拿走。
Qǐng bǎ zhèi xiē dōngxi názǒu.
Take these things away, please.

18.6 你 手 裏 拿着 甚麼？
Nǐ shǒu li názhe shénme?
What are you holding in your hand?

Now compare:

18.7 你 能 帶 多少 行李？
Nǐ néng dài duōshǎo xíngli?
How much luggage are you allowed to take?

18.8 你 能 拿 多少 行李？
Nǐ néng ná duōshǎo xíngli?
How much luggage can you carry?

"帶 dài" in 〈18.7〉 means "to take with" and "拿 ná" in 〈18.8〉 means "to carry" (physically).
See also "送 sòng" and "帶 dài" at entry 85.

19. 倒是……可是 dàoshi ... kěshi

X 倒是 Y 可是 Z, X dàoshi Y kěshi Z
X = A clause introducing the topic
Y = A clause providing the comment
Z = A clause stating something contrary to Y

Normally we use this pattern in four ways:
(1) + dàoshi +, kěshi −
(2) + dàoshi −, kěshi +
(3) *− dàoshi +, kěshi −
(4) − dàoshi −, kěshi +
"+" = positive meaning
"−" = negative meaning
* Indicates that "不 bù" cannot be used here. Only words that have negative meaning are used.

19.1 她 好看(+) 倒是 好看(+)，可是 我 不 喜歡(−) 她。
Tā hǎokàn(+) dàoshi hǎokàn(+), kěshi wǒ bù xǐhuan(−) tā.
She's good-looking all right, but I don't like her.

19.2 今天 涼快(+) 倒是 不 涼快(−)，可是 晴天(+)。
Jīntian liángkuai(+) dàoshi bù liángkuai(−), kěshi qíngtian(+).
Although the weather isn't cool today, it's a fine day.

19.3 貴(−) 倒是 不 貴(+)，可是 我 不 喜歡(−) 那 個 顏色。
Guì(−) dàoshi bú guì(+), kěshi wǒ bù xǐhuan(−) nèi ge yánsè.
It isn't that it's expensive. It's the colour that I don't like.

19.4 他 窮(−) 倒是 窮(−)，可是 很 能幹(+)。
Tā qióng(−) dàoshi qióng(−), kěshi hěn nénggàn(+).
Although he is poor, he is very capable.

Note these two points:
(1) Often we can simply use either "倒 dào" or "是 shì" instead of "倒是 dàoshi".
(2) Instead of using "可是 kěshi", we can also use "就是 jiùshi", "不過 búguò", or "但是 dànshi".

20. 到 dào (after verbs)

Typical errors:

Bring it over here.
拿 這裏 來。
Ná zhèli lái.

I thought of you yesterday.
昨天 我 想 你。
Zuótian wǒ xiǎng nǐ.

Note: This sentence would be correct if "想 xiǎng" were used in the sense of "miss", not in the sense of "thought of".

Correct usage:

拿到 這裏 來。
Nádào zhèli lái.

昨天 我 想到 你 了。
Zuótian wǒ xiǎngdào nǐ le.

The resultative complement "到 dào" means "arrive", "reach", and the noun that follows it can be a place, time, person, extent, etc. There are two points to be noted:
(1) Since "到 dào" means "arrive", "reach", the resultative verbs formed with "到 dào" necessarily involve the idea of an action which moves from one point to another.

20.1 你 看到 哪兒 了？
Nǐ kàndào nǎr le?
How far did you read?

20.2 他們 把 禮物 送到 她 家 了。
Tāmen bǎ lǐwù sòngdào tā jiā le.
They delivered the gift to her home.

20.3 他 昨天 工作到 半夜。
Tā zuótian gōngzuòdào bànyè.
He worked until midnight last night.

20.4 包裹 寄到 美國 了 嗎？
Bāoguǒ jìdào Měiguó le ma?
Has the parcel arrived in the States yet?

(2) "Verb + 到 dào" also indicates the successful conclusion of an action.

20.5 我 最後 才 接到了 我的 朋友。
Wǒ zuìhòu cái jiēdàole wǒde péngyou.
I finally managed to meet my friend.

20.6 那 本 書 我 找了 半 天 才 找到。
Nèi běn shū wǒ zhǎole bàn tiān cái zhǎodào.
I looked for the book for a long time before I found it.

Note the semantic differences between verbs with the resultative complement "到 dào" and those without it.

20.7 包裹 寄了 嗎？
Bāoguǒ jìle ma?
Has the parcel been mailed yet?

20.8 包裹 寄到了 嗎？
Bāoguǒ jìdàole ma?
Has the parcel arrived (i.e. the result of mailing) yet?

20.9 他 想了 一會兒 才 想到 你。
Tā xiǎngle yìhuǐr cái xiǎngdào nǐ.
He thought for a little while before he thought of you.

20.10 他 剛 買了 那 本 書。
Tā gāng mǎile nèi běn shū.
He just bought that book.

20.11 他 剛 買到了 那 本 書。
Tā gāng mǎidàole nèi běn shū.
He just managed to buy that book.

21. 的 de (after adjectives)

Typical errors:

very big house
很 大 房子
hěn dà fángzi

good-looking girl
好看 女孩子
hǎokàn nǚháizi

She is a beautiful person.
她 是 一 個 美的 人。
Tā shì yí ge měide rén.

Correct usage:

很 大的 房子
hěn dàde fángzi

好看 的 女孩子
hǎokàn de nǚháizi

她 是 一 個 美人。
Tā shì yí ge měirén.

"的 de" is a particle with a neutral tone.

(1) Normally we do not use "的 de" when we are modifying a noun with a one-syllable adjective.

One-syllable Adjective + Noun without "的 de".

Example:

21.1	美人 měi rén	beautiful person
21.2	好人 hǎo rén	good guy
21.3	紅花兒 hóng huār	red flower
21.4	貴書 guì shū	expensive book

When we use such adverbs of degree as "很 hěn", "太 tài", "非常 fēicháng", etc. to emphasize an adjective (one syllable), "的 de" is required.

21.5 十分 貴的 車
shífēn guìde chē
very expensive car

21.6 非常 紅的 花兒
fēicháng hóngde huār
extremely red flower

21.7 太 難的 問題
tài nánde wèntí
extremely difficult question

(2) "的 de" is usually required when we are modifying a noun with a two-syllable (or more) adjective.

Examples:

21.8 舒服的 椅子
shūfude yǐzi
comfortable chair

21.9 用功 的 學生
yònggōng de xuésheng
hardworking student

However, "的 de" is not normally used for set phrases with two-syllable adjectives.

21.10 老實 人
lǎoshi rén
honest person

21.11 積極 分子
jījí fènzǐ
active elements

21.12 偉大 領袖
wěidà lǐngxiù
great leader

21.13 重要 情況
zhòngyào qíngkuàng
important circumstances

22. 定約會 dìng yuēhuì, 掛號 guàhào, 約 yuē

Typical errors:

I've a date with my girl friend today.
我 今天 跟 我 女 朋友 有 一 個 掛號。
Wǒ jīntian gēn wǒ nǚ péngyou yǒu yí ge guàhào.

Have you made an appointment with your doctor?
你 跟 醫生 定 約會 了 嗎？
Nǐ gēn yīshēng dìng yuēhuì le ma?

Correct usage:

我 今天 跟 我 女 朋友 定了 個 約會。
Wǒ jīntiān gēn wǒ nǚ péngyou dìngle ge yuēhuì.

你 跟 醫生 掛號 了 嗎？
Nǐ gēn yīshēng guàhào le ma?

"定約會 dìng yuēhuì" means "make a date or appointment". We do not use it for medical appointments.

22.1 對不起，我 得 取消 我們 的 約會。
Duìbuqǐ, wǒ děi qǔxiāo wǒmen de yuēhuì.
I'm sorry. I have to cancel our appointment.

22.2 今天 下午 我 有 個 約會。
Jīntian xiàwǔ wǒ yǒu ge yuēhuì.
I have an appointment this afternoon.

"約 yuē" also means "make a date or appointment". Sometimes we use it to mean "invite".

22.3 我 約了 我 女 朋友 去 看 電影。
Wǒ yuēle wǒ nǚ péngyou qù kàn diàngyǐng.
I've invited my girl friend to see a movie.

22.4 我 跟 張 先生 約了 談 生意。
Wǒ gēn Zhāng xiānsheng yuēle tán shēngyi.
I've a business appointment with Mr. Zhang.

22.5 請 你 約 他 來 我 這兒 吃 晚飯。
Qǐng nǐ yuē tā lái wǒ zhèr chī wǎnfàn.
Please invite him to come to my place for dinner.

"掛號 guàhào" literally means "to have a registration number" (at a hospital or post office). We use it for making a medical appointment or registering a letter.

22.6 你 跟 醫生 掛號了 嗎？
Nǐ gēn yīshēng guàhàole ma?
Have you made an appointment with your doctor?

22.7 我 要 掛 眼科。*
Wǒ yào guà yǎnkē.
I want to make an appointment for an eye examination.

22.8 你的 信 要 掛號 不要？
Nǐde xìn yào guàhào búyào?
Do you want to register your letter?

*Since "掛號 guàhào" is a verb-object compound, its general object "號 hào" can be replaced by a definite object, i.e. "眼科 yǎnkē".

23. 東西 dōngxi and 事情 shìqing

Typical error:

He can't manage those matters.
他 辦不了 那 些 東西。
Tā bànbuliǎo nèi xiē dōngxi.

Correct usage:

他 辦不了 那 些 事情。
Tā bànbùliǎo nèi xiē shìqing.

"東西 dōngxi" means "things". Generally it refers to physical objects, but we can also use it for abstract things.

23.1 他 昨天 去 買 東西 了。
Tā zuótian qù mǎi dōngxi le.
He went shopping yesterday.

23.2 我們 有沒有 吃的 東西?
Wǒmen yǒuméiyǒu chīde dōngxi?
Do we have anything to eat?

23.3 我 沒 東西 可 寫。
Wǒ méi dōngxi kě xiě.
I don't have anything to write about.

"事情 shìqing" means "matter", "affair", "thing", "business".

23.4 我 有 太 多 事情 要 做。
Wǒ yǒu tài duō shìqing yào zuò.
I have too many things to do.

23.5 事情 就是 這樣 發生 的。
Shìqing jiùshi zhèiyàng fāshēng de.
Things just happened this way.

24. 都 dōu

Typical errors:

All the boys like me.
都　男孩子　喜歡　我。
Dōu nánháizi xǐhuan wǒ.

Not all my friends are Americans.
不　都　朋友　是　美國人。
Bù dōu péngyou shì Měiguórén.

Correct usage:

男孩子　都　喜歡　我。
Nánháizi dōu xǐhuan wǒ.

朋友　不　都　是　美國人。
Péngyou bù dōu shì Měiguórén.

"都 dōu" is an adverb. Basically, there are three points to remember:

(1) "都 dōu" is used *after* nouns and *before* verbs, adjectives and adverbs. Its semantic function is to "totalize" the noun that precedes it. Hence, it conveys the idea of "all".

24.1 我們　都　去　中國。
Wǒmen dōu qù Zhōngguó.
We are all going to China.

24.2 學生　都　很　累。
Xuésheng dōu hěn lèi.
The students are all tired.

24.3 你　每天　都　說　中國話　嗎？
Nǐ měitian dōu shuō Zhōngguóhuà ma?
Do you speak Chinese everyday?

24.4 她的　郵票　都　是　我　給　的。
Tāde yóupiào dōu shì wǒ gěi de.
All her stamps were given to her by me.

(2) When "都 dōu" is used in questions, it acts as a plural marker.

24.5 你 都 去 甚麼 地方 了？
Nǐ dōu qù shénme dìfang le?
What places did you go to?

24.6 你 都 想 吃 些 甚麼？
Nǐ dōu xiǎng chī xiē shénme?
What dishes would you like to have?

Now Compare:

24.7 你 看了 甚麼 書？
Nǐ kànle shénme shū?
What book(s) have you read?

24.8 你 都 看了 甚麼 書？
Nǐ dōu kànle shénme shū?
What books have you read?

The difference between 〈24.7〉 and 〈24.8〉 is that the latter clearly indicates plurality (of books, in this instance) whereas the former could be a case of either singularity or plurality.

(3) "都 dōu" means "already".

24.9 飯 都 做好了， 你 還 走？
Fàn dōu zuòhǎole, nǐ hái zǒu?
Why are you leaving? The rice is already cooked.

24.10 都 十二 點 了。
Dōu shíèr diǎn le.
It's already twelve o'clock.

24.11 他 都 七十 歲 了。
Tā dōu qīshí suì le.
He's already seventy years old.

For the usage of 都 in "連……都" pattern, see entry 56.

25. 對不起 duìbuqǐ, 請問 qǐngwèn, 勞駕 láojià, 麻煩您 máfan nín

Typical error:

Excuse me, where do you work?
對不起， 您 在 哪兒 工作？
Duìbuqǐ, nín zài nǎr gōngzuò?

Correct usage:

請問， 您 在 哪兒 工作？
Qǐngwèn, nín zài nǎr gōngzuò?

"對不起 duìbuqǐ" means "I'm sorry", "sorry", "pardon me", "excuse me". It is normally used as an apology.

25.1 對不起， 我 來 晚了。
Duìbuqǐ, wǒ lái wǎnle.
Sorry I'm late.

25.2 對不起， 打攪 你們 了。
Duìbuqǐ, dǎjiǎo nǐmen le.
I'm sorry to have bothered you.

25.3 對不起， 我 不 能 幫 你。
Duìbuqǐ, wǒ bù néng bāng nǐ.
Sorry, I can't help you.

"請問 qǐngwèn" means "may I inquire" or "excuse me". It is used to ask questions or seek information in a polite way.

25.4 請問， 去 北京 車站 怎麼 走？
Qǐngwèn, qù Běijīng Chēzhàn zěnme zǒu?
Excuse me, could you tell me the way to the Beijing Railway Station?

25.5 請問， 電影 幾 點 開演？
Qǐngwèn, diàngyǐng jǐ diǎn kāiyǎn?
What time will the movie start, please?

25.6 請問， 今天 星期 幾？
Qǐngwèn, jīntiān xīngqī jǐ?
Excuse me, what day is it today?

"勞駕 láojià" literally means "trouble you". It is a polite way of making requests, seeking information and asking people to step aside.

25.7 勞駕， 給 我(一)個 菜單。
Láojià, gěi wǒ(yí)ge càidān.
Can I have the menu, please?

25.8 勞駕， 郵局 在 哪兒？
Láojià, yóujú zài nǎr?
Excuse me, where is the post office?/
Can you tell me where the post office is?

25.9 勞駕， 讓 我們 過去。
Láojià, ràng wǒmen guòqu.
Please let us through.

Note: The difference between "請問 qǐngwèn" and "勞駕 láojià" is that the former is always followed by a question while the latter is either a question or a statement.
"麻煩您 máfan nín" literally means "trouble you". We use it to make requests or seek information. It is similar to "勞駕 láojià" (excuse me).

25.10 麻煩 您 把 門 關上。
Máfan nín bǎ mén guānshang.
Could you close the door please?

25.11 麻煩 您， 去 長城 飯店 怎麼 走？
Máfan nín, qù Chángchéng Fàndiàn zěnme zǒu?
Excuse me, could you tell me the way to the Great Wall Hotel?

25.12 麻煩 您， 替 我 問 她 好。
Máfan nín, tì wǒ wèn tā hǎo.
Please give my regards to her.

26. 對 duì and 跟 gēn

As preposition/coverbs, "對 duì" means "to", "face" and "跟 gēn" means "with". The basic distinction between "對 duì" and "跟 gēn" is that the former (對 duì) suggests a one-way relationship between the speaker and the listener, i.e. speaker– – – –→ listener; whereas the latter (跟 gēn) suggests a two-way relationship, i.e. speaker ←– – – – –→ listener.

26.1 他 對/跟 我 説 他 不 去 旅行 了。
Tā duì/gēn wǒ shuō tā bú qù lǚxíng le.
He told me that he is not going on the trip.

26.2 我 要 跟 你 商量 一下 那 件 事。
Wǒ yào gēn nǐ shāngliang yíxia nèi jiàn shì.
I'd like to talk with you about the matter.

"對 duì" is unacceptable here.

26.3 我 要 跟 你 談談。
Wǒ yào gēn nǐ tántan.
I want to have a word with you.

"對 duì" is unacceptable here.

26.4 他 常 對 聽衆 講話。
Tā cháng duì tīngzhòng jiǎnghuà.
He often talks before an audience.

"跟 gēn" is not used here.

26.5 他 對 我 很 好。
Tā duì wǒ hěn hǎo.
He treats me very well./He is very kind to me.

26.6 他 跟 我 很 好。
Tā gēn wǒ hěn hǎo.
He's on good terms with me.

26.7 他 對 我 很 嚴格。
Tā duì wǒ hěn yángé.
He's very strict with me.

"跟 gēn" is not used here.

27. 多 duō (before verbs and nouns)

Typical errors:

I borrowed five hundred dollars more than needed.
我 借 多了 五百 塊 錢。
Wǒ jiè duōle wǔbǎi kuài qián.

There are many people in Hong Kong.
香港 有 多 人。
Xiānggǎng yǒu duō rén.

Correct usage:

我 多 借了 五百 塊 錢。
Wǒ duō jièle wǔbǎi kuài qián.

香港 有 很多 人。
Xiānggǎng yǒu hěnduō rén.

(1) "多 duō" means "much" or "more" when it is used before verbs.

27.1 請 多 練習 四 聲。
Qǐng duō liànxí sì shēng.
Please practise your four tones more.

27.2 他 昨天 晚上 是 多 喝了 (一) 點兒。
Tā zuótian wǎnshang shì duō hēle (yì) diǎnr.
He had a little too much to drink last night.

27.3 請 你們 多 說、 多 聽。
Qǐng nǐmen duō shuō, duō tīng.
Please speak more and listen more.

(2) "多 duō" means "many" or "much" when it is used before nouns. Such adverbs as "很 hěn", "太 tài", "好 hǎo", etc. are used together with "多 duō" to modify nouns.

27.4 她 有 很多 時間。
Tā yǒu hěnduō shíjiān.
She has a lot of time.

27.5 他 買了 好 多 金子。
Tā mǎile hǎo duō jīnzi.
He bought a lot of gold.

27.6 看， 這麼 多 蘋果。
Kàn, zhème duō píngguǒ.
Look, so many apples.

28. 二 èr and 兩 liǎng

Although "二 èr" and "兩 liǎng" both mean "two", the distinction between them is a clear one.

(1) "二 èr" is used in numerical calculations.

Examples:

28.1 12 點 shíèr diǎn twelve o'clock

28.2 22 èrshièr twenty-two

28.3 92.2 jiǔshièr diǎn èr ninety-two point two

However both "二 èr" and "兩 liǎng" can be used for a digit in the hundreds place or higher.

28.4 200 èr/liǎng bǎi two hundred

28.5 222 èr/liǎng bǎi èrshièr two hundred twenty-two

28.6 20,000 èr/liǎng wàn twenty thousand

(2) "兩 liǎng" is used whenever we want to say two of anything or anyone. The pattern is "liǎng + Measure + Noun".

28.7 兩 個 人
liǎng ge rén
two persons

28.8 兩 條 魚
liǎng tiáo yú
two fish

28.9 兩 架 飛機
liǎng jià fēijī
two airplanes

28.10 兩 點 鐘
liǎng diǎn zhōng
two o'clock

29. 飯 fàn, 米 mǐ, 菜 cài

Typical error:

I suppose this dish is "sweet and sour pork".
這 個 飯 是 "咕咾 肉" 吧？
Zhèi ge fàn shì "gǔlǎo ròu" ba?

Correct usage:

這 個 菜 是 "咕咾 肉" 吧？
Zhèi ge cài shì "gǔlǎo ròu" ba?

"飯 fàn" has three meanings: (1) Normally it refers to "cooked rice". (2) It means "food" or "cuisine" when it is modified by proper nouns. However this usage is less common than "菜 cài". (3) It also means "meal".

29.1 中國 飯 人人 愛 吃。
Zhōngguó fàn rénrén ài chī.
Everybody likes Chinese food.

29.2 台灣 米 做的 飯 真 香。
Táiwān mǐ zuòde fàn zhēn xiāng.
Taiwan rice (when cooked) is really tasty.

29.3 早飯、 午飯、 晚飯， 一 天 吃 三 頓 飯。
Zǎofàn, wǔfàn, wǎnfàn, yì tiān chī sān dùn fàn.
We have three meals a day — breakfast, lunch and dinner.

"米 mǐ" means "rice" (raw).

29.4 每 月 配給 三十 斤 米。
Měi yuè pèijǐ sānshi jīn mǐ.
The monthly ration is thirty catties of rice.

29.5 每 一 粒 米 都 不 該 浪費。
Měi yí lì mǐ dōu bù gāi làngfèi.
We should not waste a single grain of rice.

"菜 cài" can be used in four ways:

(1) It is a term for vegetables in general. A more common term is "蔬菜 shūcài".

29.6 你 喜歡 種 甚麼 菜？
Nǐ xǐhuan zhòng shénme cài?
What kind of vegetables do you like to grow?

29.7 多 吃 菜， 少 吃 肉。
Duō chī cài, shǎo chī ròu.
Eat more vegetables, and less meat.

(2) It is used for "food" or "cuisine".

29.8 川菜、 京菜， 我 都 喜歡。
Chuāncài, Jīngcài, wǒ dōu xǐhuan.
I like both Sichuan and Beijing food.

(3) It is used for "dish".

29.9 三 個 菜， 一 個 湯， 夠不夠？
Sān ge cài, yí ge tāng, gòubugòu?
Are three dishes and one soup enough?

29.10 這 個 菜 用 中文 怎麼 說？
Zhèi ge cài yòng Zhōngwén zěnme shuō?
What do you call this dish in Chinese?

(4) It is used in a number of names of vegetables.

29.11 白菜 báicài Chinese cabbage

29.12 菠菜 bōcài spinach

29.13 洋白菜 yángbáicài cabbage

29.14 芹菜 qíncài celery

30. 放假 fàngjià and 假期 jiàqī

Typical errors:

We'll have a holiday tomorrow.
我們 明天 有 放假。
Wǒmen míngtiān yǒu fàngjià.

How was your holiday?
你的 放假 怎麼樣？
Nǐde fàngjià zěnmeyàng?

Correct usage:

我們 明天 放假。
Wǒmen míngtiān fàngjià.

你的 假期 過得 怎樣？
Nǐde jiàqī guòde zěnyàng?

"放假 fàngjià" means "to have a vacation or holiday". It is used as a verb-object compound and cannot be used as a noun.

30.1 放假 的 時候， 你 喜歡 做 甚麼？
Fàngjià de shíhou, nǐ xǐhuan zuò shénme?
What do you like to do when you are on vacation?

30.2 你們 放 多 久的 假？
Nǐmen fàng duō jiǔde jià?
How long will your vacation be?

"假期 jiàqī" means "vacation or holiday". We can also use "假 jià" for vacation or leave.

30.3 張 先生 在 度假 (期)。
Zhāng xiānsheng zài dùjià (qī).
Mr. Zhang is on vacation.

30.4 明天 是 甚麼 假期？
Míngtiān shì shénme jiàqī？
What holiday is it tomorrow?

30.5 你們 去年 是 在 哪兒 度的 假？
Nǐmen qùnián shì zǎi nǎr dùde jià?
Where did you spend your holiday last year?

30.6 我 明天 請假。
Wǒ míngtiān qǐngjià.
I'll ask for leave tomorrow.

31. 方便 fāngbiàn and 順便 shùnbiàn

Typical error:

Will you buy me some stamps when you go out?
你 出去 的 時候， 方便 替 我 買 幾 張 郵票，
Nǐ chūqu de shíhou, fāngbiàn tì wǒ mǎi jǐ zhāng yóupiào,
好 嗎？
hǎo ma?

Correct usage:

你 出去 的 時候， 順便 替 我 買 幾 張 郵票，
Nǐ chūqu de shíhou, shùnbiàn tì wǒ mǎi jǐ zhāng yóupiào,
好 嗎？
hǎo ma?

"方便 fāngbiàn" means "convenient". It is usually used as an adjective, although it can also be used as a noun.

31.1 要是 對 你 方便 的話， 我 現在 就 來。
Yàoshi duì nǐ fāngbiàn dehuà, wǒ xiànzài jiù lái.
If it is convenient for you, I'll come over now.

The pattern "……的話 ... de huà" means "if".

31.2 東京的 地鐵 真 方便。
Dōngjīngde dìtiě zhēn fāngbiàn.
Tokyo's subways are really convenient.

"順便 shùnbiàn" can only be used adverbially. It is used in two situations:

Situation A: Taking the opportunity of doing A, one tries to do B at the same time.

Situation B: One is going to do A and someone asks one to do B for him at the same time.

31.3 去 北京 出差 的 時候， 我 順便 到 故宮
Qù Běijīng chūchāi de shíhou, wǒ shùnbiàn dào Gùgōng
去 看了看。
qù kànlekàn.
While on a business trip to Beijing, I went to visit the Imperial Palace.

31.4 請 你 順便 把 門 關上。
Qǐng nǐ shùnbiàn bǎ mén guānshang.
Please shut the door after you.

32. 剛才 gāngcái and 剛 (剛) gāng(gāng)

"剛才 gāngcái" means "just a moment ago".

32.1 他　剛才　來過。
Tā gāngcái láiguo.
He came just a moment ago.

32.2 你　剛才　去　哪兒　了？
Nǐ gāngcái qù nǎr le?
Where have you just been?

"剛(剛) gāng (gāng)" has three meanings:

(1) It means "just".

32.3 你　剛　從　美國　來，一定　還　不　熟悉　這裏　的　情形。
Nǐ gāng cóng Měiguó lái, yídìng hái bù shúxi zhèli de qíngxing.
Since you just came from the States, you are certainly not familiar with the local situation.

(2) It means "just now".

32.4 你　進來　的　時候，他　剛　走。
Nǐ jìnlai de shíhou, tā gāng zǒu.
He left just as you came in.

(3) It means "exactly".

32.5 你的　體重　剛剛　六十　公斤。
Nǐde tǐzhòng gānggāng lìushí gōngjīn.
Your weight is exactly sixty kilos.

33. 給 gěi (after verbs)

Typical errors:

He wrote us a letter.
他 寫 我們 一 封 信。
Tā xiě wǒmen yì fēng xìn.

Did you buy her a bicycle?
你 買 她 一 輛 自行車 嗎？
Nǐ mǎi tā yí liàng zìxíngchē ma?

Correct usage:

他 寫給 我們 一 封 信。
Tā xiěgěi wǒmen yì fēng xìn.

你 買給 她 一 輛 自行車 嗎？
Nǐ mǎigěi tā yí liàng zìxíngchē ma?

When "給 gěi" (give) is used after a verb(i.e. as a post verb), it bears the meaning "to" or "for". The noun which comes after the verb is the indirect object of the verb.

33.1 請 把 鑰匙 交給 她。
Qǐng bǎ yàoshi jiāogěi tā.
Please give her the key.

33.2 他們 把 錢 還給 你 了 嗎？
Tāmen bǎ qián huángěi nǐ le ma?
Did they give you back the money?

33.3 請 講給 我 聽。
Qǐng jiǎnggěi wǒ tīng.
Tell me, please.

33.4 小 張 送給 他 女 朋友 幾 朵 玫瑰花。
Xiǎo Zhāng sònggěi tā nǚ péngyou jǐ duǒ méiguìhuā.
Little Zhang gave his girlfriend some roses.

Some commonly used "Verb-gěi" compounds are as follows:

33.5 賣給 màigěi sell to

33.6 還給 huángěi return to

33.7 交給 jiāogěi hand something to

33.8 遞給 dìgěi pass something to

34. 跟 gēn and 也 yě

Typical errors:

Let's eat and talk.
我們 吃飯 跟 談話 吧。
Wǒmen chīfàn gēn tánhuà ba.

I also like swimming.
也 我 喜歡 游泳。
Yě wǒ xǐhuan yóuyǒng.

Correct usage:

我們 一邊 吃 一邊 談 吧。
Wǒmen yìbiān chī yìbiān tán ba.

Note: The pattern "yìbiān ... yìbiān ..." either means "on the one hand ..., on the other hand ..." or "doing two things at the same time".

我 也 喜歡 游泳。
Wǒ yě xǐhuan yóuyǒng.

"跟 gēn" means "and" or "with". However, "跟 gēn" normally cannot be used to join two verbs, clauses or sentences as in English. We use it mainly to connect pronouns, nouns and nominal expressions.

34.1 我 跟 我 太太 都 是 廣東人。
Wǒ gēn wǒ tàitai dōu shì Guǎngdōngrén.
Both my wife and I are Cantonese.

34.2 我 喜歡 研究 中國的 過去、 現在 跟 將來。
Wǒ xǐhuan yánjiu Zhōngguóde guòqù, xiànzài gēn jiānglái.
I like to study China's past, present and future.

34.3 這 是 我 在 香港 買的 照相機 跟 電子 錶。
Zhèi shì wǒ zài Xiānggǎng mǎide zhàoxiàngjī gēn diànzǐ biǎo.
This is the camera and the electronic watch that I bought in Hong Kong.

"也 yě" means "also", "too", "as well". It cannot be used before nouns as the English "also" is used since it is an adverb.

34.4 **A:** 我 數學 得了 一百 分。
Wǒ shùxué déle yìbǎi fēn.
I scored 100% in mathematics.

B: 我 也 得了 一百 分。
Wǒ yě déle yìbǎi fēn.
Me too!/I also scored 100%.

34.5 我 也 不 會 開車。
Wǒ yě bú huì kāichē.
I also don't know how to drive.

34.6 他 孩子 愛 吃 香蕉， 也 愛 吃 蘋果。
Tā háizi ài chī xiāngjiāo, yě ài chī píngguǒ.
His children love bananas and (also love) apples.

34.7 他 去過 美國、 英國， 也 去過 中國。
Tā qùguo Měiguó, Yīngguó, yě qùguo Zhōngguó.
He's been to the States, England, and (also) China.

35. 夠 gòu

Typical error:

He's not fast enough.
他 快得 不 夠。
Tā kuàide bú gòu.

Correct usage:

他 不 夠 快。
Tā bú gòu kuài.

"夠 gòu" means "enough" or "sufficient". It can be used in several ways.

(1) "Noun + 夠" (English equivalent = "enough + Noun")

35.1 我們的 時間 夠不夠？
Wǒmende shíjiān gòubugòu?
Do we have enough time?

(2) "夠 + Adjective" (English equivalent = "Adjective + enough")

35.2 他 寫的 字 已經 夠 好 了。
Tā xiěde zì yǐjīng gòu hǎo le.
His characters are already good enough.

(3) "夠 + Verb" (English equivalent = "enough to + Verb")

35.3 農民 已經 夠 吃 夠 穿 了。
Nóngmín yǐjīng gòu chī gòu chuān le.
The farmers already have enough to eat and wear.

(4) "Verb + 夠" (English equivalent = "Verb + enough")

35.4 這 些 東西 我 已經 聽 夠 了。
Zhèi xiē dōngxi wǒ yǐjīng tīng gòu le.
I've heard enough of this stuff.

36. 關於 guānyú and 對於 duìyú

"關於 guānyú" is a preposition (or coverb). It introduces the scope of an activity or subject. Hence, it is used in the sense of "about" or "concerning". It is used in two ways:

(1) It is used adverbially before the subject of a sentence.

36.1 關於 他的 事，我 不 願意 再 談了。
Guānyú tāde shì, wǒ bú yuànyi zài tánle.
I don't want to talk about his things any more.

36.2 關於 中國 經濟，她 知道 的 比 我 多。
Guānyú Zhōngguó jīngji, tā zhīdao de bǐ wǒ duō.
She knows more about the Chinese economy than I do.

(2) It is used to modify the object of a sentence. In this usage, it always takes the structural particle "的 de" before the object it modifies.

36.3 我 要 給 你們 講 一 個 關於 中國 古代 的 故事。
Wǒ yào gěi nǐmen jiǎng yí ge guānyú Zhōngguó gǔdài de gùshi.
I want to tell you a story about ancient China.

36.4 這 是 一 本 關於 打 乒乓球 的 書。
Zhèi shì yì běn guānyú dǎ pīngpāngqiú de shū.
This is a book on table tennis.

"對於 duìyú" is also a preposition. Its main function is to transpose the object of a sentence to a preverbal position, thus stressing the object. It is used in two ways:

(1) It is used adverbially before or after the subject of a sentence.

36.5 對於 修理 汽車，他 很 有 經驗。
Duìyú xiūlǐ qìchē, tā hěn yǒu jīngyàn.
He is very experienced in fixing cars.

36.6 我們 對於 這 個 問題 還 得 多 研究 研究。
Wǒmen duìyú zhèi ge wèntí hái děi duō yánjiu yánjiu.
We still have to study this problem a bit more.

(2) It is used to modify a noun. In this usage, it always takes the structural particle "的 de" before the noun it modifies.

36.7 這 就是 我 對於 這 件 事情 的 看法。
Zhèi jiùshi wǒ duìyú zhèi jiàn shìqing de kànfǎ.
This is my viewpoint on this matter.

36.8 對於 老 人 的 服務 還是 很 不 夠 的。
Duìyú lǎo rén de fúwù háishi hěn bú gòu de.
Service for the elderly is still very inadequate.

37. 過 guo

We use "Verb-guo" in two distinct situations:

Situation A: "過 guo" is used after a verb to indicate a completed action, which can be a past, present or future one.

37.1 他 吃過飯 就 回家了。
Tā chīguofàn jiù huíjiāle.
He ate and went back home.

37.2 你 剛才 喝過 咖啡 嗎？
Nǐ gāngcái hēguo kāfēi ma?
Did you just drink coffee?

37.3 明天 打過 網球 以後，一起 去 公園 好 嗎？
Míngtian dǎguo wǎngqiú yǐhòu, yìqǐ qù gōngyuán hǎo ma?
How about going to the park after we play tennis tomorrow?

Situation B: "過 guo" is used after a verb or an adjective to indicate an experience, past or conditional.

37.4 你 開過 飛機 嗎？
Nǐ kāiguo fēijī ma?
Have you ever flown an airplane before?

37.5 我 小 時候 窮過。
Wǒ xiǎo shíhou qióngguo.
I suffered poverty when I was young.

37.6 要是 你 去過 桂林，就 一定 會 愛上 那兒的 山 水。
Yàoshi nǐ qùguo Guìlín, jiù yídìng huì àishang nàrde shān shuǐ.
If you have ever been to Guilin, you would certainly love the mountains and waters there.

For a comparison of "了 le" and "過 guo", see entry 53.

38. 還是 háishi and 或者(或是)huòzhě (huòshi)

Typical error:

Do we go tomorrow or next week?
我們　明天　去　或者　下　星期　去？
Wǒmen míngtian qù huòzhě xià xīngqī qù?

Correct usage:

我們　明天　去　還是　下　星期　去？
Wǒmen míngtian qù háishi xià xīngqī qù?

Although " 還是 háishi" and " 或者 huòzhě" both mean "or", the distinction between them is a clear one. " 還是 haíshi" can be used as a question word whereas " 或者 huòzhě" cannot. When " 還是 háishi" is not used as a question word, it is equivalent to " 或者 huòzhě".

38.1 她　喜歡　吃　魚，還是　喜歡　吃　雞？
Tā xǐhuan chī yú, háishi xǐhuan chī jī?
Does she like fish or chicken?

38.2 他們　八　點　到，還是　九　點　到？
Tāmen bā diǎn dào, háishi jiǔ diǎn dào?
Are they coming at eight or nine?

38.3 你　是　學生　，還是　老師？
Nǐ shì xuésheng, háishi lǎoshī?
Are you a student or a teacher?

38.4 紅的　還是／或者　綠的，都　可以。
Hóngde háishi/huòzhě lǜde, dōu kěyǐ.
The red one or the green one, either is fine.

" 還是 háishi" can also be used in the following two ways:

(1) " 還是 háishi" means "still, nevertheless".

38.5 他　雖然　很　累，可是　還是　把　功課　做完了。
Tā suīrán hěn lèi, kěshi háishi bǎ gōngkè zuòwánle.
Although he was tired he finished his homework anyway.

(2) " 還是 háishi" means "had better".

38.6 你 還是 明天 再 走 吧。
Nǐ háishi míngtian zài zǒu ba.
You'd better leave tomorrow.

38.7 她 還是 學 中文 好。
Tā háishi xué Zhōngwén hǎo.
It's better for her to study Chinese.

Note: "還是 … 好 háishi … hǎo" is used to indicate one course of action is better than another.

We use " 或者 huòzhě" in two ways:

(1) It means "or".

38.8 你 寫信 或者 打 電話 給 他，都 可以。
Nǐ xiěxìn huòzhě dǎ diànhuà gěi tā, dōu kěyǐ.
It doesn't matter if you write to him or call him.

38.9 你 可以 穿 這 件 大衣 或者 那 件。
Nǐ kěyǐ chuān zhè jiān dàyī huòzhě nèi jiàn.
You can wear either this overcoat or that one.

(2) It means "perhaps, maybe".

38.10 或者 明天 會 更 好。
Huòzhě míngtian huì gèng hǎo.
Maybe tomorrow will be better.

38.11 你 或者 不 應該 那樣 對 她。
Nǐ huòzhě bù yīnggaī nèiyàng duì tā.
Perhaps you shouldn't treat her like that.

39. 會 huì

Typical error:

I can't go back because I don't have a car.
我 不 會 回去，因爲 沒 車。
Wǒ bú huì huíqu, yīnwèi méi chē.

Correct usage:

我 不能 回去，因爲 沒 車。
Wǒ bùnéng huíqu, yīnwèi méi chē.

We normally use the modal verb "會 huì" in three ways (Note: modal verbs are verbs which express ability, possibility, suggestion, etc.):

(1) It means "know how to".

39.1 我 會 說 中國話。
Wǒ huì shuō Zhōngguóhuà.
I can speak Chinese.

39.2 我 不 會 用 電腦。
Wǒ bú huì yòng diànnǎo.
I can't operate a computer.

(2) It indicates a possibility, either past or future.

39.3 下午 會 下雨。
Xiàwǔ huì xiàyǔ.
It could rain this afternoon.

39.4 他 不 會 不 說 再見 就 走了。
Tā bú huì bù shuō zàijiàn jiù zǒule.
He couldn't have left without saying goodbye (to us).

39.5 他們 會 準時 到 嗎？
Tāmen huì zhǔnshí dào ma?
Will they arrive on time?

(3) It means "good at" when it is preceded by such adverbs of degree as "很 hěn", "最 zuì", "真 zhēn", and "太 tài".

39.6 她 真 會 說話。
Tā zhēn huì shuōhuà.
She is really eloquent.

39.7 他 很 會 講 笑話。
Tā hěn huì jiǎng xiàohua.
He's very good at telling jokes.

For a comparative analysis of "能 néng", "會 huì" and "可以 kěyǐ", see entry 63.

40. Inclusives and exclusives with 哪兒 nǎr, 甚麼 shénme, 誰 shéi

Typical error:

I like everybody.
我 喜歡 誰 都。
Wǒ xǐhuan shéi dōu.

Correct usage:

我 誰 都 喜歡。
Wǒ shéi dōu xǐhuan.

To express in Chinese inclusive or exclusive ideas such as "everybody" and "nobody", "everywhere" and "nowhere", and "everything" and "nothing", we use question words (nǎr, shénme, shéi) followed by the word "都 dōu" or "也 yě".

"哪兒都/也 + Verb"

40.1 在 紐約 市中心， 哪兒 都 是 高樓 大厦。
Zài Niǔyuē shìzhōngxīn, nǎr dōu shì gāolóu dàxià.
Skyscrapers are everywhere in downtown New York.

40.2 在 上海 的 時候， 我 哪兒 都 没 去。
Zài Shànghǎi de shíhou, wǒ nǎr dōu méi qù.
I didn't go anywhere when I was in Shanghai.

"甚麼都/也 + Verb"

40.3 今天 我 甚麼 都 没 買。
Jīntian wǒ shénme dōu méi mǎi.
I didn't buy anything today.

40.4 昨天 我 甚麼 報 也 没 看。
Zuótian wǒ shénme bào yě méi kàn.
I didn't read any newspapers yesterday.

"誰都/也 + Verb"

40.5 在 學校裏， 誰 都 認識 他。
Zài xuéxiàoli, shéi dōu rènshi tā.
Everybody in the school knows him.

40.6 那 本 書，我 誰 也 不 借。
Nèi běn shū, wǒ shéi yě bú jiè.
I won't lend that book to anybody.

40.7 我 誰 都 不 告訴。
Wǒ shéi dōu bú gàosu.
I won't tell anybody.

Note: The negative marker "不 bù" is placed after the question words.

Attention should be made that the main verb in an inclusive or exclusive sentence is positioned *after* the question words, *not before*. This differs from English patterns of inclusives and exclusives.

41. 家 jiā and 房子 fángzi

Typical error:

Please come to my place when you have time.
請 有 空 到 我的 房子 來 玩兒。
Qǐng yǒu kòng dào wǒde fángzi lái wánr.

Correct usage:

有 空 請 到 我 家 來 玩兒。
Yǒu kòng qǐng dào wǒ jiā lái wánr.

The English equivalent to " 家 jiā" is "home", which may refer to either the place where one lives or one's close family and one's self.

41.1 這兒 就是 我們 家。
Zhèr jiùshi wǒmen jiā.
This is our home.

41.2 在 東方 或者 西方，自己的 家 最 好。
Zài dōngfāng huòzhě xīfāng, zìjǐde jiā zuì hǎo.
East, west, home's best.

41.3 你們 家 有 幾 個 人？
Nǐmen jiā yǒu jǐ ge rén?
How many people are there in your family?

41.4 我們 家 前頭 有 棵 大 樹。
Wǒmen jiā qiántou yǒu kē dà shù.
There's a big tree in front of our house.

Unlike " 家 jiā", " 房子 fángzi" refers only to the physical structure within which one lives. It is translated as "house" or "building" in English.

41.5 這 就是 我們 新 買 的 房子。
Zhèi jiùshi wǒmen xìn mǎi de fángzi.
This is our newly bought house.

41.6 我們的 房子* 後頭 有 一 所 大 房子。
Wǒmende fángzi hòutou yǒu yì suǒ dà fángzi.
There's a big house in the back of our house.

*" 家 jiā" is also acceptable here.

42. 借 jiè, 借給 jiègěi, 跟……借 gēn ... jiè

Typical error:

I borrowed five hundred dollars from him.
我 借了 五百 塊 錢 跟 他。
Wǒ jièle wǔbǎi kuài qián gēn tā.

Correct usage:

我 跟 他 借了 五百 塊 錢。
Wǒ gēn tā jièle wǔbǎi kuài qián.

"借 jiè" can either mean "borrow" or "lend". The exact meaning is normally determined by the context.

42.1 今天 放假， 所以 圖書館 不 借 書。
Jīntian fàngjià, suǒyǐ túshūguǎn bú jiè shū.
Since it's a holiday today, the library is closed (isn't lending books).

42.2 我 可以 借 你的 鋼筆 嗎？
Wǒ kěyǐ jiè nǐde gāngbǐ ma?
May I borrow your pen?

"借給 jiègěi" means "lend". We can also use "借 + Noun + 給 + Noun" for "lending something to someone".

42.3 我 借給了 他 一 本 字典。
Wǒ jiègěile tā yì běn zìdiǎn.
I lent him a dictionary.

42.4 她 借了 她的 雨衣 給 我。
Tā jièle tāde yǔyī gěi wǒ.
She lent her raincoat to me.

"跟 gēn + Noun + 借 jiè" means "borrow from".

42.5 他 爲甚麼 要 跟 你 借 自行車？
Tā wèishénme yào gēn nǐ jiè zìxíngchē?
Why does he want to borrow the bicycle from you?

42.6 我 要 跟 政府 借 些 錢。
Wǒ yào gēn zhèngfǔ jiè xiē qián.
I want to/am going to borrow some money from the government.

Note: When we use the pattern "跟……借 gēn ... jiè", it is necessary to place the lender after "跟 gēn" and the object borrowed after "借 jiè". If we don't want to mention the lender in the sentence, the expression "跟……借" should not be used. "借 jiè" is used instead.

For example:

42.7 我 借了 一 些 信紙 跟 信封。
Wǒ jièle yì xiē xìnzhǐ gēn xìnfēng.
I borrowed some writing paper and envelopes.

43. 接 jiē and 接到 jiēdào

Typical error:

I didn't receive that letter.
那　封　信，我　没　接。
Nèi fēng xìn, wǒ méi jiē.

Correct usage:

那　封　信，我　没　接到。
Nèi fēng xìn, wǒ méi jiēdào.

Basically, there are two distinct points to be noted; one is a semantic point while the other relates to parts of speech.

(1) We use "接 jiē" for "answering" a phone call and "接到 jiēdào" for "receiving" a phone call.

43.1 請　你　接　一下　電話。
Qǐng nǐ jiē yíxià diànhuà.
Please answer the phone.

43.2 她　接到了　一　個　長途　電話。
Tā jiēdàole yí ge chángtú diànhuà.
She received a long-distance call.

43.3 那　封　電報，我　没　接到。
Nèi fēng diànbào, wǒ méi jiēdào.
I didn't receive that telegram.

(2) "接 jiē" is an *action verb* whereas "接到 jiēdào" is a *resultative verb*. When both are used in the sense of "meet", "接到 jiēdào" means "manage to meet".

43.4 我　昨天　去　機場　接　她，可是　没　接到。
Wǒ zuótian qù jīchǎng jiē tā, kěshi méi jiēdào.
I went to the airport to meet her yesterday, but I failed to meet her.

43.5 你　接到　飛機　了　嗎？*
Nǐ jiēdào fēijī le ma?
Did you manage to meet your friend at the airport?

*Naturally this expression does not mean to meet the airplane, but rather the person who travelled by airplane. We can also say "去接車 qù jiē chē" (go to meet someone at the railway station) or "去接船 qù jiē chuán" (go to meet someone at the dock).

44. 記得 jìde and 記住 jìzhu

"記得 jìde" means "to remember" (i.e. recall from memory).

44.1 你 還 記得 我 嗎？
Nǐ hái jìde wǒ ma?
Do you still remember me?

44.2 你 記不記得 從前 見過 她？
Nǐ jìbujìde cóngqián jiànguo tā?
Do you remember seeing her before?

"記住 jìzhu" means "bear in mind". Since it is a resultative verb, it can be used in the potential form, i.e. "記得住 jìdezhù" (able to remember) and "記不住 jìbuzhù" (unable to remember).

44.3 你 記得住 這麼 多 名字 嗎？
Nǐ jìdezhù zhème duō míngzi ma?
Can you remember (memorize) all these names?

44.4 記住， 我們 晚上 一塊兒 下館子。
Jìzhu, wǒmen wǎnshang yíkuàr xiàguǎnzi.
Remember (put in your memory), we're going to eat out together tonight.

The distinction between "記得 jìde" and "記住 jìzhu" is shown in the diagrams below:

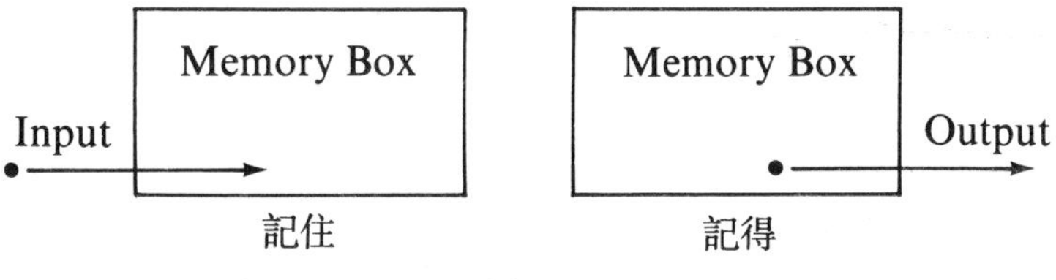

"記住" refers to committing something to memory, whereas "記得" refers to recalling something from memory.

45. 就 jiù

"就 jiù" has many functions when it is used as an adverb. However, only four functions will be introduced here.

(1) It indicates early occurrence or conclusion of an event or action.
Note that time words are often contained in this usage.

45.1 他 早上 五 點 半 就 出門 了。
Tā zǎoshang wǔ diǎn bàn jiù chūmén le.
He went out as early as 5:30 a.m.

45.2 她 不到 十七 歲 就 大學 畢業 了。
Tā búdào shíqī suì jiù dàxué bìyè le.
She graduated from the university even before she was seventeen years old.

45.3 你 現在 就 走 嗎？
Nǐ xiànzài jiù zǒu ma?
Are you leaving already?

(2) It indicates immediacy, in the sense of "right away" or "right after".

45.4 我 現在 就 來。
Wǒ xiànzài jiù lái.
I'm coming right away.

45.5 他 下了課 就 回家。
Tā xiàlekè jiù huíjiā.
He'll go home right after the class is over.

(3) It is used in the sense of "only".

45.6 她 就 會 說 英語。
Tā jiù huì shuō Yīngyǔ.
She speaks only English.

45.7 他們 就 (有) 一 個 孩子。
Tāmen jiù (yǒu) yí ge háizi.
They have only one child.

45.8 就 他 自己 住在 這兒 嗎？
Jiù tā zìjǐ zhùzai zhèr ma?
Does he live here just by himself?

(4) It indicates that something should not be taken too seriously. In this usage, it normally follows the pattern "A jiù A + Clause".

45.9 丢 就 丢了， 我們 下次 再 買 一 個。
Diū jiù diūle, wǒmen xiàcì zài mǎi yí ge.
If it's lost, it's lost. We'll get another one next time.

45.10 行 就 行， 不 行 就 算了！
Xíng jiù xíng, bù xíng jiù suànle!
If it's O.K., it's fine. If not, forget it !

45.11 他 生氣 就 生氣 吧， 反正 不是 我的 錯。
Tā shēngqì jiù shēngqì ba, fǎnzhèng búshì wǒde cuò.
If he's angry, let him be angry. Anyhow it's not my fault.

46. 就 jiù and 才 cái

There are four basic differences between "就 jiù" and "才 cái".

(1) "就 jiù" indicates an early occurrence of an action while "才 cái" indicates a late occurrence of an action.

46.1 你 怎麼 現在 就 走？
Nǐ zěnme xiànzài jiù zǒu?
How come you are leaving already?

46.2 你 怎麼 現在 才 走？
Nǐ zěnme xiànzài cái zǒu?
How come you aren't leaving until now?

46.3 我 一九四九 年 就 離開 中國 了。
Wǒ yī jiǔ sì jiǔ nián jiù líkāi Zhōngguó le.
I left China as early as 1949.

46.4 我 是 一九四九 年 以後 才 離開 中國 的。
Wǒ shì yī jiǔ sì jiǔ nián yǐhòu cái líkāi Zhōngguó de.
I didn't leave China until after 1949.

(2) When two actions are connected by "就 jiù", it indicates that the second action will take place as soon as the first one is concluded. When two actions are connected by "才 cái", it indicates that the second action will not take place until the first one is concluded.

46.5 你 做完 功課 就 可以 去 玩兒。
Nǐ zuòwán gōngkè jiù kěyǐ qù wánr.
You may go to play as soon as your homework is done.

46.6 你 做完 功課 才 可以 去 玩兒。
Nǐ zuòwán gōngkè cái kěyǐ qù wánr.
You may not go to play until your homework is done.

46.7 你 給 他 吃 糖，他 就 告訴 你。
Nǐ gěi tā chī táng, tā jiù gàosù nǐ.
He'll tell you as soon as you give him some candy.

46.8 你 給 他 吃 糖，他 才 告訴 你。
Nǐ gěi tā chī táng, tā cái gàosù nǐ.
He won't tell you until you give him some candy.

(3) "才 cái" may only indicate a small quantity or degree whereas "就 jiù" may indicate either a small or a relatively large quantity or degree, depending on where the stress is and the context.

46.9 我們 兩 個 人 才 打了 兩 隻 鳥，他 一 個
Wǒmen liǎng ge rén cái dǎle liǎng zhī niǎo, tā yí ge
人 就 打了 四 隻。
rén jiù dǎle sì zhī.
The two of us shot only two birds, but he shot as many as four by himself.

46.10 他 才 借了 一百 塊 錢。
Tā cái jièle yìbǎi kuài qián.
He only borrowed one hundred dollars.

46.11 他 就 借了 一百 塊 錢，我 怎麼 好意思 再 跟
Tā jiù jièle yìbǎi kuài qián, wǒ zěnme hǎoyìsi zài gēn
人 借？
rén jiè?
He borrowed as much as one hundred dollars. How can I have the nerve to go there to borrow too ?

Note: To indicate a relatively large quantity, we place the stress on the pronoun or the numeral which precedes "就 jiù". "就 jiù" should not be stressed in this usage.

(4) For the pattern "Time Word + Past Event", "才 cái" employs the "是……的 shì ... de" construction whereas "就 jiù" generally uses the verb suffix "了 le".

46.12 她 從 小 就 會 畫畫兒 了。
Tā cóng xiǎo jiù huì huàhuàr le.
She could paint even when she was a little child.

46.13 我 十 點 鐘 就 來了，可是 小 李 是 十一 點 半
Wǒ shí diǎn zhōng jiù láile, kěshi xiǎo Lǐ shì shíyī diǎn bàn
才 到 的。
cái dào de.
I got here at ten o'clock, but little Li didn't show up (arrive) until eleven thirty.

47. 看 kàn, 見 jiàn, 看見 kànjian

Typical errors:

I don't want to see you.
我 不 要 看 你。
Wǒ bú yào kàn nǐ.

I didn't see her.
我 没 看 她。
Wǒ méi kàn tā.

Note: "看 kàn" would be correct here in the sense of "to visit", but not in the sense of physical sight.

Correct usage:

我 不 要 看見 你。
Wǒ bú yào kànjian nǐ.

我 没 看見 她。
Wǒ méi kànjian tā.

"看 kàn" is used in several ways. It has four basic meanings, three of which are related to our physical sight. It can also appear in reduplicated form (see reduplication of verbs at entry 67).

(1) It means "look, look at".

47.1 讓 我 看看 你。
Ràng wǒ kànkan nǐ.
Let me look at you.

47.2 人 老了， 眼睛 看 不 清楚 了。
Rén lǎole, yǎnjing kàn bù qīngchu le.
When a person gets old, he can no longer see clearly.

(2) It means "watch" (games, TV, etc.) or "see" (films and plays).

47.3 我 愛 看 足球 比賽。
Wǒ ài kàn zúqiú bǐsài.
I love to watch soccer games.

47.4 你 看過 "星球 大戰" 嗎？
Nǐ kànguo "Xīngqiú Dàzhàn" ma?
Have you ever seen "Star Wars"?

(3) It means "read".

47.5 你 喜歡 看 甚麼 書？
Nǐ xǐhuan kàn shénme shū?
What kind of books do you like to read?

47.6 你 看過 《紅樓夢》 嗎？
Nǐ kànguo Hónglóumèng ma?
Have you ever read *Dream of the Red Chamber*?

(4) It means "visit or see", usually a casual visit to a friend.

47.7 我 要 到 英國 去 看 一 個 好 朋友 去。
Wǒ yào dào Yīngguó qù kàn yí ge hǎo péngyou qù.
I'm going to England to visit a good friend of mine.

47.8 他 病 的 時候， 我 去 看過 他。
Tā bìng de shíhou, wǒ qù kànguo tā.
I went to see him when he was ill.

"見 jiàn" has two primary meanings. It can also appear in reduplicated form.

(1) It means "see". It is similar to "看見 kànjian" (see).

47.9 我 不 要 見 你。
Wǒ bú yào jiàn nǐ.
I don't want to see you.

47.10 你 是 在 哪兒 見過 這 張 畫兒 的？
Nǐ shì zài nǎr jiànguo zhèi zhāng huàr de?
Where have you seen this painting before?

(2) It means "meet", "see", "call on". The meeting can either be a first meeting or a formal one.

47.11 我們 好像 在 哪兒 見過。
Wǒmen hǎoxiàng zài nǎr jiànguo.
It seems that we've met each other before.

47.12 他 要 見見 校長。
Tā yào jiànjian xiàozhǎng.
He wishes to see the headmaster.

47.13 老闆 要 見 你。
Lǎobǎn yào jiàn nǐ.
The boss wants to see you.

"看見 kànjian" means "see". It is a resultative verb.

47.14 一 看見 他， 我 就 生氣。
Yí kànjian tā, wǒ jiù shēngqì.
The minute I see him, I get angry.

47.15 誰　看不見？
Shéi　kànbujiàn?
Who can't see it?

47.16 你　看得見　那　個　飯店　嗎？
Nǐ　kàndejiàn　nèi　ge　fàndiàn　ma?
Can you see that hotel?

48. 課 kè, 班 bān, 節 jié (堂 táng)

Typical error:

How many students are there in this class?
這 個 課 有 幾 個 學生？
Zhèi ge kè yǒu jǐ ge xuésheng?

Correct usage:

這 個 班 有 幾 個 學生？
Zhèi ge bān yǒu jǐ ge xuésheng?

"課 kè" is used for "lessons" or "classes"/"periods". We do not use it to talk about the size of a class.

48.1 第一 節 課 是 早上 八 點 鐘。
Dìyī jié kè shì zǎoshang bā diǎn zhōng.
The first class/period is at 8:00 a.m.

48.2 今天 上 第三 課。
Jīntian shàng dìsān kè.
Today we are on lesson three.

"班 bān" means "class". We use it in reference to a group of students.

48.3 這 個 班 的 學生 都 有 進步。
Zhèi ge bān de xuésheng dōu yǒu jìnbù.
All the students in this class have made progress.

48.4 我們 班 明天 去 北海 公園 划船 去。
Wǒmen bān míngtian qù Běihǎi Gōngyuán huáchuán qù.
Our class is going boating in Beihai Park tomorrow.

Note: The measure word for "課 kè" (class) is "節 jié" or "堂 táng" while that for "班 bān" (class) is "個 gè".

49. 可憐 kělián and 可惜 kěxī

Typical error:

It's a pity that I wasn't able to go to the movie yesterday.
可憐 我 昨天 没 能 去 看 電影。
Kělián wǒ zuótian méi néng qù kàn diànyǐng.

Correct usage:

可惜 我 昨天 没 能 去 看 電影。
Kěxī wǒ zuótiān méi néng qù kàn diànyǐng.

Note: This sentence would be acceptable if the speaker meant "I was pitiful", but not in the sense of "It's a pity".

"可憐 kělián" means "pitiful" or "have pity on". It is used either as an adjective or a verb. We use it to express our sympathy or pity toward persons or animate objects.

49.1 這 個 孩子 真 可憐。
Zhèi ge háizi zhēn kělián.
This child is truly pitiful.

49.2 我 才 不 可憐 你 呢！
Wǒ cái bù kělián nǐ ne!
I don't feel sorry for you, not I.

49.3 你 這 個 可憐蟲！
Nǐ zhèi ge kěliánchóng!
What a poor thing you are!

"可惜 kěxī" means "it's too bad" or "it's a pity." It is used as an adjective or an adverb. We use it to indicate something regrettable.

49.4 要是 你 去不了 的 話，那 真 可惜。
Yàoshi nǐ qùbuliǎo de huà, nà zhēn kěxī.
It'll be too bad if you can't go.

49.5 可惜 他 没 考上 大學。
Kěxī tā méi kǎoshang dàxué.
Too bad he didn't pass the university entrance examination.

49.6 把 球鞋 扔了 多 可惜。
Bǎ qiúxié rēngle duō kěxī.
What a pity to throw the tennis shoes away.

50. 可以 kěyǐ

Typical error:

Can I get this book in China?
在 中國 可以 買 這 本 書 嗎？
Zài Zhōngguó kěyǐ mǎi zhèi běn shū ma?

Note: "可以買 kěyǐ mǎi" would be correct here in the sense of "be allowed to buy", but not in the sense of "be able to get".

Correct usage:

在 中國 買得到 這 本 書 嗎？
Zài Zhōngguó mǎidedào zhèi běn shū ma?

The modal verb "可以 kěyǐ" has three primary meanings.

(1) It indicates "possibility under certain conditions". However, this usage is restricted to positive sentences. Negative sentences use "能 néng".

50.1 我們 可以 走着 去 嗎？
Wǒmen kěyǐ zǒuzhe qù ma?
Can we walk there?/Is it possible for us to walk there?

50.2 可以 用 紙 作 飛機 嗎？
Kěyǐ yòng zhǐ zuò fēijī ma?
Is it possible to make airplanes from paper?

50.3 **A:** 這 間 屋子 可以 住 五 個 人 嗎？
Zhèi jiān wūzi kěyǐ zhù wǔ ge rén ma?
Can five people stay in this room?

B: 不 行。
Bù xíng.
No, they can't.

Note: A negative response to "possibility" with "可以 kěyǐ" is "不行 bù xíng" or "不成 bù chéng" rather than "不可以 bù kěyǐ".

(2) It indicates "permission to do/say something".

50.4 老師，我 可以 問 你 個 問題 嗎？
Lǎoshī, wǒ kěyǐ wèn nǐ ge wèntí ma?
Sir, may I ask you a question?

50.5 我 可以 進來 嗎？
Wǒ kěyǐ jìnlai ma?
May I come in?

50.6 我 可以 用 你們的 衛生間 嗎？
Wǒ kěyǐ yòng nǐmende wèishēngjiān ma?
May I use your bathroom?

(3) It indicates "suggestions", "requests" and "offers".

50.7 你 可以 買 些 水果 送給 她。
Nǐ kěyǐ mǎi xiē shuǐguǒ sònggěi tā.
You can/could buy her some fruit.

50.8 你 父母 可以 先 在 我們 家 住 幾 天。
Nǐ fùmǔ kěyǐ xiān zài wǒmen jiā zhù jǐ tiān.
Your parents could stay at our house for a couple of days.

50.9 你 可以 幫 我 一下 嗎？
Nǐ kěyǐ bāng wǒ yíxià ma?
Could you give me a hand?

50.10 要是 你 不 舒服， 我 可以 替 你 去 買。
Yàoshi nǐ bù shūfu, wǒ kěyǐ tì nǐ qù mǎi.
If you aren't feeling well, I could go and buy it for you.

For a comparative analysis of "會 huì", "可以 kěyǐ" and "能 néng", see entry 63.

51. 恐怕 kǒngpà and 怕 pà

Typical error:

I'm afraid of him.
我　恐怕　他。
Wǒ kǒngpà tā.

Correct usage:

我　怕　他。
Wǒ pà tā.

We use " 恐怕 kǒngpà" to mean "I'm afraid (that something might happen)" or "perhaps". We use " 怕 pà" to mean "I'm afraid of" or "fear". Sometimes " 怕 pà" can be used interchangeably with " 恐怕 kǒngpà".

51.1 這樣　做　恐怕／怕　不　行。
Zhèiyàng zuò kǒngpà / pà bù xíng.
I'm afraid this won't work.

51.2 我　恐怕／怕　他　來不了　了。
Wǒ kǒngpà / pà tā láibuliǎo le.
I'm afraid he is not able to come now.

51.3 這　個　西瓜　恐怕／怕　不　熟。
Zhèi ge xīguā kǒngpà / pà bù shóu.
I'm afraid this watermelon might not be ripe.

51.4 你　怕　學　中國字　嗎？
Nǐ pà xué Zhōngguózì ma?
Are you afraid of learning Chinese characters?

51.5 這（個）孩子　怕　生。
Zhèi (ge) háizi pà shēng.
This child is shy with strangers.

51.6 真　金　不　怕　火。
Zhēn jīn bú pà huǒ.
Genuine gold fears no fire.

52. 了 le

Typical errors:

That student worked hard at his studies.
那 個 學生 用了功 念書。
Nèi ge xuésheng yònglegōng niànshū.

From that time on, he no longer drank liquor.
從 那 時候 起，他 不 喝酒。
Cóng nèi shíhou qǐ, tā bù hējiǔ.

Correct usage:

那 個 學生 用功 念書。
Nèi ge xuésheng yònggōng niànshū.

從 那 時候 起，他 不 喝酒 了。
Cóng nèi shíhou qǐ, tā bù hējiǔ le.

This particle is one of the most commonly used "empty words" in Mandarin Chinese, especially in spoken Chinese. It is called an "empty word" because it does not have any concrete meaning in itself. We should not equate it with the English past tense, although it seems to be so at first sight.

With regard to position, "了 le" can appear in two places in a sentence. It can either appear after a verb or at the end of a sentence.

With regard to function, it has four primary usages, namely, to indicate "completed action", "a new situation", "progress so far" and "modal emphasis".

(1) "了 le" used after verbs to indicate "completed action" (past, present or future).

52.1 他 昨天 看了 一 場 電影。
Tā zuótian kànle yì chǎng diànyǐng.
He saw a movie yesterday.

52.2 我 吃了飯 了，謝謝。
Wǒ chīlefàn le, xièxie.
I've eaten, thanks.

52.3 她 明天 來了，請 她 來 見 我。
Tā míngtian láile, qǐng tā lái jiàn wǒ.
When she comes tomorrow, please ask her to come see me.

52.4 我們 下了 課 就 回家。
Wǒmen xiàle kè jiù huíjiā.
We'll go back home after class.

Note: In 〈52.3〉 and 〈52.4〉 "了 le" is used for the future actions "來 lái" (come) and "下 xià" (finish). By using "了 le" the temporal order of two future actions in a sentence is established. In other words "了 le" indicates explicitly that after the first action is completed the second action will take place.

(2) "了 le" used at the end of a sentence to indicate "a new situation".

52.5 他 喜歡 學習 中國話 了。
Tā xǐhuan xuéxí Zhōngguóhuà le.
Now he likes to study Chinese (implying he didn't like Chinese before).

52.6 她 瘦了。
Tā shòule.
She's thinner than before.

52.7 這 本 書 現在 賣 一百 塊 錢 了。
Zhèi běn shū xiànzài mài yìbǎi kuài qián le.
This book now costs one hundred dollars.

52.8 蘋果 紅起來 了。
Píngguǒ hóngqilai le.
The apples are turning red now.

52.9 她 不 學 毛筆字 了。
Tā bù xué máobǐzì le.
She is not learning calligraphy now.

(3) "Double 了 le" used with quantified objects to indicate "progress so far".

52.10 他 在 這兒 住了 三 年 了。
Tā zài zhèr zhùle sān nián le.
He's been living here for three years.

52.11 我 吃了 兩 碗 飯 了。
Wǒ chīle liǎng wǎn fàn le.
I've had two bowls of rice (so far).

Compare the use of "了 le" with "了……了 le ... le", i.e. "completed action" versus "progress so far".

52.12 我 寫了 十 個 字。
Wǒ xiěle shí ge zì.
I've written ten characters. / I wrote ten characters.

The action is fully completed.

52.13 我 寫了 十 個 字 了。
Wǒ xiěle shí ge zì le.
I've written ten characters (so far).

Although the action is also completed, it is likely to carry on in the future.

(4) "了 le" is used for "modal emphasis", e.g. in negative commands with "別 bié ", after exclamatory expressions with "太 tài", and in imperative sentences.

52.14 這 棵 樹 太 高 了。
Zhèi kē shù tài gāo le.
This tree is extremely tall.

52.15 別 忘了!
Bié wàngle!
Don't forget!

52.16 放了 它。
Fàngle tā.
Let it go.

52.17 扔了 它。
Rēngle tā.
Throw it away.

Note: When "了 le" is used for "modal emphasis" at the end of a sentence, it is generally pronounced as "啦 la".

53. 了 le and 過 guo

(1) We use "了 le" to indicate a completed action while "過 guo" indicates having experienced an event.

Compare:

53.1 他 去了 中國 兩 次。
Tā qùle Zhōngguó liǎng cì.
He's gone to China twice.

The emphasis is on the completed action "去 qù".

53.2 他 去過 中國 兩 次。
Tā qùguo Zhōngguó liǎng cì.
He's been to China twice.

The emphasis is on the experience of going to China.

(2) The negative form of "Verb-le" is "沒 + Verb" while that of "Verb-guo" is "沒 + Verb-過".

Compare:

53.3 我們 沒 唱歌。
Wǒmen méi chànggē.
We didn't sing.

53.4 我們 沒 唱過歌。
Wǒmen méi chàngguogē.
We've never sung before.

(3) When "了 le" and "過 guo" are used jointly after verbs, "過 guo" is always placed before "了 le". A verb using "過了 guole" after it is more emphatic in conveying the idea of "completion" than one using "了 le" only.

53.5 咱們 聽過了 唱片 再 走。
Zánmen tīngguole chàngpiàn zài zǒu.
We'll go after listening to the records.

53.6 誰 洗過了 澡 再 洗？
Shéi xǐguole zǎo zài xǐ?
Who would take a bath after having already bathed?

(4) "過 guo" and "了 le" are interchangeable in the following two patterns.

(a) "Verb-guo/le + Noun + le"

(b) "$Verb_1$-guo/le + Noun + $Verb_2$"

53.7 **Either** 她 今天 寫過信 了。
Tā jīntian xiěguoxìn le.

or 她 今天 寫了信 了。
Tā jīntian xiělexìn le.
She wrote letters today.

53.8 **Either** 我 是 打過 網球 才 走 的。
Wǒ shì dǎguo wǎngqiú cái zǒu de.

or 我 是 打了 網球 才 走 的。
Wǒ shì dǎle wǎngqiú cái zǒu de.
I didn't leave until after I'd played tennis.

54. 離 lí and 從 cóng

We use "離 lí" to talk about the distance between two places or two points in time, whereas we use "從 cóng" to indicate a starting point, which could be spacial, temporal or categorical.

54.1 宿舍 離 學校 不 遠。
Sùshè lí xuéxiào bù yuǎn.
The dorm is not far from the school.

54.2 離 他的 生日 還 有 兩 個 星期。
Lí tāde shēngrì hái yǒu liǎng ge xīngqī.
His birthday is two weeks from now.

54.3 她 剛 從 國外 回來。
Tā gāng cóng guówài huílai.
She just came back from abroad.

54.4 他 從 早 到 晚 地 工作。
Tā cóng zǎo dào wǎn de gōngzuò.
He works from morning till night.

54.5 從 男 到 女，從 老 到 小，都 希望
Cóng nán dào nǚ, cóng lǎo dào xiǎo, dōu xīwang
「中國 女排」勝利。
Zhōngguó Nǚpái shènglì.
Man and women, old and young alike wish the Chinese women's volleyball team victory.

55. 離不開 líbukāi and 走不開 zǒubukāi

(1) "離不開 líbukāi" is used in the sense of "unable to leave (a place)" or "unable to part with a person". "走不開 zǒubukāi" is only used in the sense of "unable to leave a place".

55.1 孩子 太 小， 離不開 父母。
Háizi tài xiǎo, líbukāi fùmǔ.
The child is too young to leave his parents.

55.2 這兒 太 忙， 我 走不開。
Zhèr tài máng, wǒ zǒubukāi.
It's too busy here; I can't leave.

55.3 他 離不開 醫院， 因爲 他 太太 快 生 孩子 了。
Tā líbukāi yīyuàn, yīnwèi tā tàitai kuài shēng háizi le.
He can't leave the hospital because his wife is about to have a baby.

(2) "離不開 líbukāi" can take an object, whereas "走不開 zǒubukāi" cannot.

55.4 校長 離不開 學校。
Xiàozhǎng líbukāi xuéxiào.
The headmaster can't leave the school.

55.5 學校 太 多 問題， 所以 校長 走不開。
Xuéxiào tài duō wèntí, suǒyǐ xiàozhǎng zǒubukāi.
Because the school has too many problems, the headmaster can't leave.

56. 連……都/也 lián ... dōu/yě

Typical error:

He doesn't even know me.
他　連　認識　我　都　不　認識。
Tā lián rènshi wǒ dōu bú rènshi.

Correct usage:

他　連　我　都　不　認識。
Tā lián wǒ dōu bú rènshi.

The pattern "連……都/也 lián ... dōu/yě" means "even".
There are two points to be noted:
(1) The main verb of the sentence appears only after the pattern "連……都/也", *not* before it. This differs from English usage.
(2) The object of emphasis, which can be a verb phrase, noun phrase or an adjective, is inserted between "連 lián" and "都 dōu" or "也 yě".

56.1 他　連　我　都　不　認識。
Tā lián wǒ dōu bú rènshi.
He doesn't even know me.

The emphasis is on "me" not "know".

56.2 他　連　太太　的　話　都　不　聽。
Tā lián tàitai de huà dōu bù tīng.
He would not even listen to his wife.

56.3 我　連　買書　也　買不起。
Wǒ lián mǎishū yě mǎibuqǐ.
I can't even afford to buy books.

56.4 連　我　開車　也　不　行。
Lián wǒ kāichē yě bù xíng.
Even if I drove it wouldn't be all right.

57. 忙甚麼 máng shénme, 不忙 bù máng, 別忙 bié máng

The expression "忙甚麼？ Máng shénme?" has two meanings. First, it means "What's the hurry?" and second, "What are you busying yourself with?"

57.1 忙 甚麼？ 請 再 坐 一會兒。
Máng shénme? Qǐng zài zuò yìhuǐr.
What's the hurry? Please stay a little longer.

57.2 你 整天 忙 甚麼？
Nǐ zhěngtiān máng shénme?
What have you been busying yourself with all day?

The expression "不忙 bù máng" means "no hurry". It is normally used before something is done with haste.

57.3 不 忙， 錢 你 甚麼 時候 方便 再 還。
Bù máng, qián nǐ shénme shíhou fāngbiàn zài huán.
No hurry, you can pay me back whenever it is convenient.

The idiom "別忙 bié máng" means "don't rush" or "take your time". It is used generally in a situation in which something is being done in a hurry. It can also mean "wait a minute".

57.4 **A:** 我 明天 把 書 還給 你。
Wǒ míngtian bǎ shū huángěi nǐ.
I'll give you back the book tomorrow.

B: 不 忙， 慢慢兒 看 吧。
Bù máng, mànmānr kàn ba.
No hurry. Take your time.

57.5 別 忙， 別 開得 太 快。
Bié máng, bié kāide tài kuài.
There's no hurry. Don't drive so fast.

57.6 別 忙， 讓 我 想一想。
Bié máng, ràng wǒ xiǎngyixiǎng.
Wait a minute. Let me think about it.

58. 沒關係 méi guānxi

Typical error:

It doesn't matter whether he's going or not.
沒 關係， 他 去不去。
Méi guānxi, tā qùbuqù.

Correct usage:

他 去不去， 沒 關係。
Tā qùbuqù, méi guānxi.

The idiom "沒關係 méi guānxi" means "it doesn't matter", "that's all right", "never mind" and "it's not important".

58.1 多 長 時間 都 沒 關係。
Duō cháng shíjiān dōu méi guānxi.
It doesn't matter how long it takes.

58.2 他 知道 不 知道 這 件 事， 沒 關係。
Tā zhīdao bu zhīdao zhèi jiàn shì, méi guānxi.
It's not important whether he knows about it or not.

58.3 **A:** 對不起，我 來 晚 了。
Duìbuqǐ, wǒ lái wǎn le.
Sorry, I'm late.

B: 沒 關係。
Méi guānxi.
That's all right.

Note: The phrase "沒(有)關係 méi (you) guānxi" means "not relevant" or "not related to". Unlike "沒關係 méi guānxi", it is not an idiom.

For example:

58.4 我 跟 他們 完全 沒 關係。
Wǒ gēn tāmen wánquán méi guānxi.
I'm totally unrelated to them.

59. Modifying relative clause + de + noun

The construction "modifier + de + noun" is one of the key links in Chinese grammar. Therefore, a thorough understanding of it is a "must" in the study of Mandarin Chinese. There are three points to note:

(1) The English equivalent to this construction is the "defining relative clause", which tells us which person or thing is being referred to.

(2) Unlike the English "defining relative clause", this construction has the modifying elements placed before the noun it refers to, *not* after it.

(3) When specifiers and measure words are used, they should be placed directly after the defining elements and before the noun they refer to.

59.1 他們 買的 電冰箱 貴。
Tāmen mǎide diànbīngxiāng guì.
The refrigerator that they bought is expensive.

59.2 昨天 跟 我 一塊兒 喝茶 的 那 個 人 是 我 弟弟。
Zuótian gēn wǒ yíkuàr hēchá de nèi ge rén shì wǒ dìdi.
The one with whom I had tea yesterday is my younger brother.

59.3 這 就是 我 第一 次 見到 她的 地方。
Zhèi jiùshi wǒ dìyī cì jiàndào tāde dìfang.
This is the place where I met her for the the first time.

60. 拿起來 náqilai and 拿上來 náshanglai

Typical error:

He picked up his pen.
他　拿上來　他的　筆　了。
Tā　náshanglai　tāde　bǐ　le.

Correct usage:

他　把　筆　拿起來　了。
Tā　bǎ　bǐ　náqilai　le.

We use "拿起來 náqilai" to talk about an action which causes a lying object to move upward. Therefore it is used in the sense of "to pick up". A similar expression, "撿起來 jiǎnqilai", is used for "picking up some small objects from the floor". "拿上來 náshanglai" is used to talk about an action which causes an object to move from a lower position to a higher one. Therefore it is used in the sense of "to bring something up".
The distinction between "拿起來 náqilai" and "拿上來 náshanglai" is illustrated in the following two diagrams:

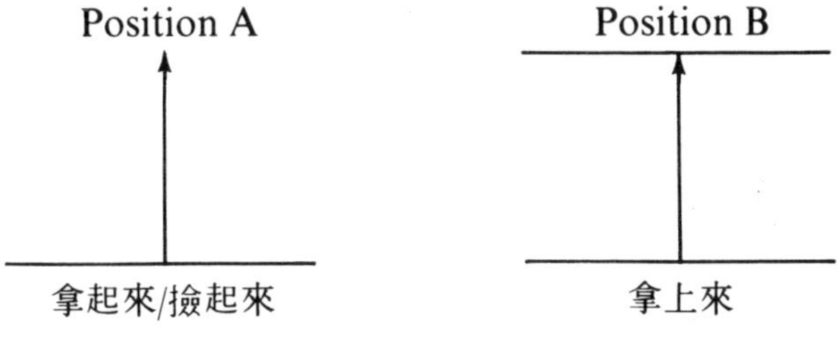

60.1 他　拿起　筆　來　寫了　三　封　長　信。
Tā　náqǐ　bǐ　lai　xiěle　sān　fēng　cháng　xìn.
He picked up his pen and wrote three long letters.

Note: The direct object (that which is picked up) is placed between "起 qǐ" and "來 lái" when the "把 bǎ" pattern is not used.

60.2 同志們，　把　槍　拿起來。
Tóngzhìmen,　bǎ　qiāng　náqilai.
Comrades, pick up your guns.

60.3 把　紙　撿起來。
Bǎ　zhǐ　jiǎnqilai.
Pick up the paper (from the floor).

60.4 把 碗 拿上來， 放在 桌子 上面。
Bǎ wǎn náshanglai, fàngzai zhuōzi shàngmian.
Bring your bowl up and put it on the table.

60.5 你 上來 的 時候， 請 把 毛巾 拿上來。
Nǐ shànglai de shíhou, qǐng bǎ máojīn náshanglai.
When you come up, please bring the towel with you.

61. 呢 ne and 嗎 ma

(1) When "嗎 ma" is placed at the end of a declarative sentence, it turns the sentence into a *general question*. It need not be so with "呢 ne".

Compare:

61.1 他 在 北京 嗎？
Tā zài Běijīng ma?
Is he in Beijing?

61.2 這 件 事 可 不 小 呢！
Zhèi jiàn shì kě bù xiǎo ne!
This is no small matter!

"呢 ne" is used here for emphasis.

(2) "呢 ne" cannot be used for a *yes-no question*, that is, a question which can be answered with either "yes" or "no". However, there is no such restriction on the use of "嗎 ma".

(3) "呢 ne" can appear at the end of a *special question*, that is, a question that employs such question words as "誰 shéi" (who), "甚麼 shénme" (what), and "哪兒 nǎr" (where). We cannnot use "嗎 ma" in a *special question*.

61.3 你 爲甚麼 不 去 呢？
Nǐ wèishénme bú qù ne?
Why aren't you going?

61.4 她 不 喜歡 誰 呢？
Tā bù xǐhuan shéi ne?
Who doesn't she like?

Note: When "呢 ne" is used in a *special question*, it functions as a modal particle. Although a *special question* would still be acceptable without using "呢 ne", the presence of "呢 ne" could soften the tone of the question.

(4) When "呢 ne" and "嗎 ma" appear simultaneously in a sentence, "呢 ne" alway precedes "嗎 ma".

61.5 他們 還沒 吃飯 呢 嗎？
Tāmen háiméi chīfàn ne ma?
Haven't they eaten yet?

61.6 張 經理 在 見 外賓 呢 嗎？
Zhāng jīnglǐ zài jiàn wàibīn ne ma?
Is Mr. Zhang, the manager, receiving foreign guests?

62. 能 néng

Typical error:

Tomorrow you can come to my place first.
你 明天 能 先 到 我 這裏 來。
Nǐ míngtian néng xiān dào wǒ zhèli lái.

Correct usage:

你 明天 可以 先 到 我 這裏 來。
Nǐ míngtiān kěyǐ xiān dào wǒ zhèli lái.

"能 néng" along with "會 huì" and "可以 kěyǐ", is a commonly used modal verb. It has four basic meanings:

(1) It indicates "a general ability" to do something.

62.1 你 今天 晚上 能 來 嗎？
Nǐ jīntian wǎnshang néng lái ma?
Can you come tonight?

62.2 小 王 很 能 做事。
Xiǎo Wáng hěn néng zuòshì.
Little Wang is very capable.

62.3 他 不 能 游泳。
Tā bù néng yóuyǒng.
He can't swim.

(2) It indicates "possibility under certain conditions".

62.4 我們 不 能 走着 去 嗎？
Wǒmen bù néng zǒuzhe qù ma?
Can't we walk there?

62.5 不 能 用 紙 做 飛機。
Bù néng yòng zhǐ zuò fēijī.
It's not possible to make airplanes from paper.

62.6 這 間 屋子 能 住 五 個 人。
Zhèi jiān wūzi néng zhù wǔ ge rén.
This room can accomodate five people.

(3) It indicates "a functional ability or characteristic".

62.7 絲 能 做 衣服。
Sī néng zuò yīfu.
Silk can be used to make clothes.

62.8 這 架 飛機 能 在 高空 飛行。
Zhèi jià fēijī néng zài gāokōng fēixíng.
This airplane is capable of flying at high altitudes.

62.9 水 在 攝氏 零 度 能 變成 冰。
Shuǐ zài Shēshì líng dù néng biànchéng bīng.
Water turns into ice at 0℃.

(4) It indicates "permission or request".

62.10 我 能 進來 嗎?
Wǒ néng jìnlai ma?
May I come in?

62.11 我們 能 抽煙 嗎?
Wǒmen néng chōuyān ma?
May we smoke?

62.12 **A:** 你 能 幫 我 一下 嗎?
Nǐ néng bāng wǒ yíxià ma?
Can you give me a hand?

B: 可以。
Kěyǐ.
Sure.

Note: A positive response to "permission or request" with "能 néng" is "可以 kěyǐ" rather than "能 néng".

63. 能 néng, 會 huì, 可以 kěyǐ

Almost every beginner of Chinese is confused by these three modal verbs (i.e. verbs expressing ability, possibility, suggestion, etc.). The cause for much confusion is a simple one. When these three modal verbs are translated into English, they are often rendered as "can" which is also a modal verb. Therefore when an English speaking student wants to translate into Chinese a sentence with "can", he finds himself at a complete loss as to which verb to employ: "會 huì", "能 néng", "可以 kěyǐ", or even the potential form of the resultative verb.

Beginners of Chinese are advised to master the primary meanings of each of these three modal verbs at the outset, and learn the advanced points at a later stage of their studies.

(1) Primary meanings of "會 huì", "可以 kěyǐ", "能 néng": "會 huì" has two primary meanings. First, it means "know how to". Second, it indicates "a past or future possibility".

63.1 我 會 用 筷子。
Wǒ huì yòng kuàizi.
I can (know how to) use chopsticks.

63.2 他們 倆 會 結婚 嗎？
Tāmen liǎ huì jiéhūn ma?
Will they get married?

"可以 kěyǐ" has two primary meanings. First, it indicates "possibility under certain conditions". Second, it means "permission or request".

63.3 人類 可以 征服 太空 嗎？
Rénlèi kěyǐ zhēngfú tàikōng ma?
Is it possible for mankind to conquer the space?

63.4 我 可以 借 你的 筆 用 一下 嗎？
Wǒ kěyǐ jiè nǐde bǐ yòng yíxià ma?
May I borrow your pen for a minute?

"能 néng" has one primary meaning. It indicates "a general ability", usually a physical one.

63.5 你 能 舉起 我 嗎？
Nǐ néng jǔqi wǒ ma?
Can you lift me up?

63.6 今天 我 不 能 説話
Jīntian wǒ bù néng shuōhuà.
I can't (am not able to) speak today.

(2) Although both "能 néng" and "會 huì" can be used in the sense of "know how to", we tend to use "會 huì" more often than "能 néng".
(3) When "能 néng" is used in the sense of "permission or request", the negative response is not "不能 bù néng" but "不可以 bù kěyǐ".
(4) When "可以 kěyǐ" is used in the sense of "possibility", the negative form is not "不可以 bù kěyǐ" but "不能 bùnéng". "會 huì", "能 néng" and "可以 kěyǐ" are compared in the diagram below:

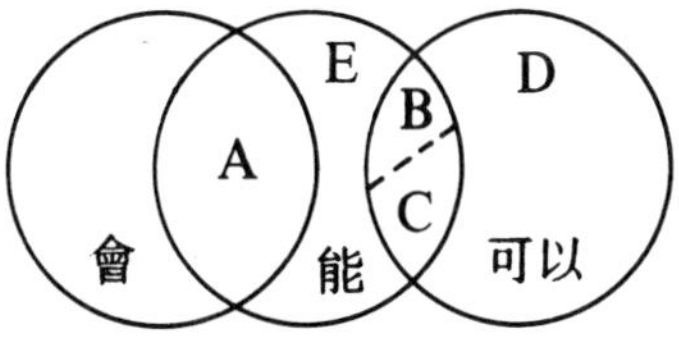

A = ability in the sense of "know how to" ("會" is more common than "能")
B = permission/request(use "能"or "可以")
C = possibility (use "能" or "可以")
D = permission not granted (use "不可以")
E = impossibilty (use "不能")

64. 年 nián, 月 yuè, 星期 xīngqī, 天 tiān

Typical errors:

What's the date today?
今天 是 哪 天？
Jīntian shì nǎ tiān?

今天 是 甚麼 天？
Jīntian shì shénme tiān?

Correct usage:

今天 是 幾 號？
Jīntiān shì jǐ hào?

When we talk about dates and times, we place the largest time element first, followed by smaller elements. Hence, "年 nián" (year) precedes "月 yuè" (month), "月 yuè" precedes "星期 xīngqī" (week), and so on.

64.1 一 九 四 九 年 十月 一號 (日) 上午 十 點 (時)。
Yī jiǔ sì jiǔ nián Shíyuè Yīhào (rì) shàngwǔ shí diǎn (shí).
10:00 a.m., October 1, 1949.

Time words in parentheses are used in writing or formal speech.

64.2 你 星期 幾 考試？
Nǐ xīngqī jǐ kǎoshì?
On what day is your exam?

64.3 今天 (是) 幾 號？
Jīntian (shì) jǐ hào?
What's the date today?

64.4 現在 (是) 幾 月？
Xiànzài (shì) jǐ yuè?
What month is it now?

64.5 你的 生日 是 幾 月 幾 號？
Nǐde shēngrì shì jǐ yuè jǐ hào?
When is your birthday?

When we come to past and future dates in Chinese, students of Chinese are often confused and at times stutter. The cause of stuttering and/or confusion is due to differences between the Chinese and the Westerner's conception of time.

The time axes below show this distinction.

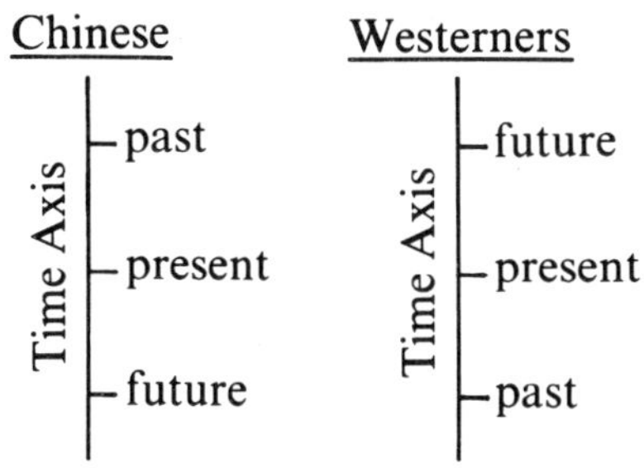

Hence,
"上星期 Shàngxīngqī" is "last week" (*not* next week)
"下星期 Xiàxīngqī" is "next week" (*not* last week)
"上午 Shàngwǔ" is "morning " (*not* afternoon)
"下午 Xiàwǔ" is "afternoon" (*not* morning)

With regard to "前天 qiántian" (day before yesterday) and "後天 hòutian" (day after tomorrow), "前 qián" should not be interpreted as "in front of" (indicating future), but should be interpreted as "before or ago", while "後 hòu" is not used in the sense of "behind" or "back" (indicating past) but rather it is used in the sense of "after" or "later".

65. 唸 niàn, 看 kàn, 讀 dú

Typical error:

I read a magazine yesterday.
我　昨天　唸了　一　本　雜誌。
Wǒ　zuótian　niànle　yì　běn　zázhì.

Correct usage:

我　昨天　看了　一　本　雜誌。
Wǒ　zuótian　kànle　yì　běn　zázhì.

The difference between " 唸 niàn" and " 看 kàn" is that " 唸 niàn" means "read aloud" and " 看 kàn" means "read". We also use " 唸 niàn" in the sense of "study" or "attend school".

65.1　你　今天　唸書　了　嗎？
Nǐ　jīntian　niànshū　le　ma?
Have you studied today?

65.2　他　没　唸過　大學。
Tā　méi　niànguo　dàxué.
He didn't go to college.

65.3　請　你　把　她的　信　唸唸／唸出來　。
Qǐng　nǐ　bǎ　tāde　xìn　niànnian / niànchulai.
Please read her letter out loud.

65.4　你　今天　看書　了　嗎？
Nǐ　jīntian　kànshū　le　ma?
Have you read any books today?

65.5　你　看了　她的　來　信　嗎？
Nǐ　kànle　tāde　lái　xìn　ma?
Have you read her letter?

65.6　她　看得懂　中文　，可是　不　會　說　。
Tā　kàndedǒng　Zhōngwén,　kěshi　bú　huì　shuō.
She reads Chinese, but she doesn't speak it.

We use " 讀 dú" in three ways:

(1) It means "read" and is equivalent to " 看 kàn".

65.7 我 不是 每天 都 讀／看 報紙。
Wǒ búshi měitian dōu dú / kàn bàozhǐ.
I don't read the newspaper everyday.

65.8 這 本 是 孩子 最 愛 讀／看 的 書。
Zhèi běn shì háizi zuì ài dú / kàn de shū.
This is the most popular book among children.

(2) It means "read aloud" and is equivalent to " 唸 niàn".

65.9 請 跟着 我 讀／唸。
Qǐng gēnzhe wǒ dú / niàn.
Please say it after me.

65.10 請 把 這 個 句子 讀／唸 給 我 聽。
Qǐng bǎ zhèi ge jùzi dú / niàn gěi wǒ tīng.
Please read this sentence to me.

(3) It means "study" or "attend school" and is equivalent to " 唸 niàn".

65.11 他 讀書／唸書 很 用功 。
Tā dúshū / niànshū hěn yònggōng.
He works hard at his studies.

65.12 她 没 讀／唸完 大學 就 開始 工作 了。
Tā méi dú / niànwán dàxué jiù kāishǐ gōngzuò le.
She started working before she finished college.

66. 派 pài, 送 sòng, 寄 jì

Typical error:

Her parents have sent her to China to study.
她 父母 寄/派 她 到 中國 留學了。
Tā fùmǔ jì/pài tā dào Zhōngguó liúxuéle.

Correct usage:

她 父母 送 她 到 中國 去 留學 了。
Tā fùmǔ sòng tā dào Zhōngguó qù liúxué le.

"派 pài" means "to send (officially)" or "to appoint". It can only be used to talk about people.

66.1 中國 每 年 都 派 學生 出國 學習。
Zhōngguó měi nián dōu pài xuésheng chūguó xuéxí.
Every year China sends students to study abroad.

66.2 我 派 她 當 班長。
Wǒ pài tā dāng bānzhǎng.
I'll appoint her to be the class monitor.

"送 sòng" means "to send" or "to deliver". We can use it to refer to either people or things.

66.3 我 多 派了 一 個 人 去 送信。
Wǒ duō pàile yí ge rén qù sòngxìn.
I sent an extra person to deliver letters.

66.4 父母 都 願意 送 自己 的 孩子 上 大學。
Fùmǔ dōu yuànyi sòng zìjǐ de háizi shàng dàxué.
All parents wish to send their children to college.

See also "送 sòng" and "帶 dài" at entry 85.

"寄 jì" means "to send (by mail)" or "remit". It cannot be used to talk about people.

66.5 我 常 給 他 寄 錢。
Wǒ cháng gěi tā jì qián.
I often send (remit) him money.

66.6 你 把 信 寄了 嗎?
Nǐ bǎ xìn jìle ma?
Have you mailed the letter?

67. 碰 pèng, 碰見(碰到) pèngjian (pèngdào), 碰上 pèngshang

"碰 pèng" means "to touch" or "to bump against".

67.1 別 碰 我！
Bié pèng wǒ!
Don't touch me!

67.2 他 把 頭 碰在 門 上 了。
Tā bǎ tóu pèngzai mén shang le.
He bumped his head on the door.

"碰 pèng" can also be used in the sense of "try one's luck" or "take one's chance".

67.3 我 是 去 碰碰 運氣 的。
Wǒ shì qù pèngpeng yùnqi de.
I went to try my luck.

"碰見 pèngjian" is normally used in the sense of "bump into" or "run into someone".

67.4 我 没 碰見 她。
Wǒ méi pèngjian tā.
I didn't bump into her.

67.5 你 猜 我 碰見 誰 了？
Nǐ cāi wǒ pèngjian shéi le?
Guess who I bumped into?

"碰到 pèngdào" means "run into" (a person) or "come up against" (problems, obstacles, etc.).

67.6 前 幾 天 我 碰到 你的 老師 了。
Qián jǐ tiān wǒ pèngdào nǐde lǎoshī le.
I ran into your teacher the other day.

67.7 我 碰到了 (一)些 困難。
Wǒ pèngdàole (yì)xiē kùnnan.
I've encountered some difficulty.

"碰上 pèngshang" can also be used in the sense of "bump into someone". It also means "to meet with" (unexpected events).

67.8 我 碰上了 一 個 熟 朋友。
Wǒ pèngshangle yí ge shú péngyou.
I bumped into an old friend.

67.9 在　路上　他們　碰上了　大　雨。
Zài lùshàng tāmen pèngshangle dà yǔ.
They met with heavy rain on the way.

Note: To say "run into" in the sense of "to collide", normally we use "撞上 zhuàngshang" or "撞 + resultative complement". For example: "兩輛車撞上了 liǎng liàng chē zhuàngshangle" (two cars ran into each other). "他被車撞倒了 Tā bèi chē zhuàngdǎole" (He was knocked down by a car). "To be run over by a car" is "被車軋了 bèi chē yàle".

68. 碰見（遇見）pèngjian (yùjian) and 見面 jiànmiàn

Typical error:

I met a woman yesterday.
我 昨天 見面 一 個 女人。
Wǒ zuótian jiànmiàn yí ge nǚrén.

Correct usage:

我 昨天 碰見／遇見了 一 個 女人。
Wǒ zuótian pèngjian / yùjianle yí ge nǚrén.

"碰見 pèngjian" differs from "見面 jiànmiàn" in that "碰見 pèngjian" is used in the sense of "meet (someone) unexpectedly" while "見面 jiànmiàn" in the sense of "meet" or "see". Unlike "碰見 pèngjian", "見面 jiànmiàn" cannot take a noun after it.

68.1 我 從來 没 碰見過 這樣 的 人。
Wǒ cónglái méi pèngjianguo zhèiyàng de rén.
I've never met such a person before.

68.2 你們 常 見面 嗎？
Nǐmen cháng jiànmiàn ma?
Do you see each other a lot?

68.3 我 是 在 街 上 遇見 他 的。
Wǒ shì zài jiē shang yùjian tā de.
I met him in the street.

68.4 他 和 他 太太 一 年 才 見 一 次 面。
Tā hé tā tàitai yì nián cái jiàn yí cì miàn.
He sees his wife only once a year.

68.5 我 想 我們 以前 没 見過面。
Wǒ xiǎng wǒmen yǐqián méi jiànguomiàn.
I don't think we've met before.

69. 輕 qīng and 薄 báo

Typical error:

He had a light breakfast.
他 吃了 一 個 輕 早飯。
Tā chīle yí ge qīng zǎofàn.

Correct usage:

他 早飯 吃了 很 少。
Tā zǎofàn chīle hěn shǎo.

To talk about "light clothes or meals" we do not use "輕 qīng" which means "light" (in weight). Instead "薄 báo" (thin) is used for clothes and "吃得很少 chīde hěn shǎo" (eat very little) for meals.

69.1 他 平常 早飯 吃得 很 少。
Tā píngcháng zǎofàn chīde hěn shǎo.
He usually takes a light breakfast.

69.2 夏天 穿 薄 衣服 舒服。
Xiàtian chuān báo yīfu shūfu.
It's comfortable to wear light clohes in the summer.

69.3 我 喜歡 吃 薄餅 。
Wǒ xǐhuan chī báobǐng.
I like (to eat) thin pancake.

69.4 油 比 水 輕。
Yóu bǐ shuǐ qīng.
Oil is lighter than water.

70. 請 qǐng and 請客 qǐngkè

Typical error:

Has she invited you?
她 請客了 你 嗎？
Tā qǐngkèle nǐ ma?

Correct usage:

她 請 你 了 嗎？
Tā qǐng nǐ le ma?

"請 qǐng" means "to invite". It is also used in the sense of "to treat someone to something". The general pattern is "Noun + qǐng + Noun + Verb phrase".

70.1 他們 請 我 到 他們 家 去 玩兒。
Tāmen qǐng wǒ dào tāmen jiā qù wánr.
They invited me to go to their home for a visit.

70.2 我 請 你 看 電影。
Wǒ qǐng nǐ kàn diànyǐng.
I'll treat you to a movie.

70.3 她 請 我 吃 糖。
Tā qǐng wǒ chī táng.
She offered me some candy.

"請客 qǐngkè" is a verb-object compound. Its literal meaning is "to invite guests". It is, therefore, used in the sense of "to give a party" or in situations where one would say "It's my treat".

70.4 今天 晚上 誰 請客？
Jīntian wǎnshang shéi qǐngkè?
Who's giving a dinner party tonight?

70.5 我們 去 打 枱球 去， 我 請客。
Wǒmen qù dǎ táiqiú qù, wǒ qǐngkè.
Let's go play snooker. It's my treat.

71. 請 qǐng and 請問 qǐngwèn

Typical error:

Do you have some time to spare, please?
請　你　有　空兒　嗎？
Qǐng　nǐ　yǒu　kòngr　ma?

Correct usage:

請問，　你　有　空兒　嗎?
Qǐngwèn,　nǐ　yǒu　kòngr　ma?

"請 qǐng" means "please". In this sense, it is generally followed by a verb or an adjective. It is normally used in the imperative to indicate a polite request.

71.1 請坐，　請坐。
Qǐngzuò,　qǐngzuò.
Please take a seat.

71.2 請　安静。
Qǐng　ānjìng.
Be quiet please.

71.3 請進，　請進。
Qǐngjìn,　qǐngjìn.
Please do come in.

"請問 qǐngwèn" means "may I inquire" or "excuse me". It is always followed by a question.

71.4 請問，　到　郵局　去　怎麼　走？
Qǐngwèn,　dào　yóujú　qù　zěnme　zǒu?
Excuse me, could you tell me how to get to the post office?

71.5 請問，　你　是　哪　國　人？
Qǐngwèn,　nǐ　shì　něi　guó　rén?
May I ask what nationality you are?

71.6 請問，　現在　幾　點　了？
Qǐngwèn,　xiànzài　jǐ　diǎn　le?
Could you tell me the time, please?

See also "請問 qǐngwèn", "勞駕 láojià" and "麻煩您 máfan nín" at entry 25.

72. 請 qǐng, 問 wèn, 叫 jiào

Typical error:

Ask her to come here.
問 她 來 這兒。
Wèn tā lái zhèr.

Correct usage:

請/叫 她 來 這兒。
Qǐng/Jiào tā lái zhèr.

"請 qǐng" means "to ask" or "to invite". It is a polite form of expression.

72.1 麻煩 你， 請 她 來 一下。
Máfan nǐ, qǐng tā lái yíxià.
Would you please ask her to come here for a minute?

72.2 他 請 我 當 班長。
Tā qǐng wǒ dāng bānzhǎng.
He asked me to be the class monitor.

"問 wèn" is used only in the sense of "to ask (questions)" or "to inquire about".

72.3 她 問了 我 一 個 私人 問題。
Tā wènle wǒ yí ge sīrén wèntí.
She asked me a personal question.

72.4 他 問 我 北京 車站 在 哪。
Tā wèn wǒ Běijīng Chēzhàn zài nǎr.
He asked me where the Beijing Railway Station was.

"叫 jiào" means "to ask", "to order" or "to tell". When we want to say "ask" in the sense of "to require or call for" in an informal way, we use "叫 jiào", not "請 qǐng" which is a formal and polite form.

72.5 昨天 他 叫 我 出去 玩兒。
Zuótian tā jiào wǒ chūqu wánr.
He asked me to go out yesterday.

72.6 叫 他們 過來。
Jiào tāmen guòlai.
Ask them to come over.

72.7 (是) 誰 叫 你 進來 的？
(Shì) Shéi jiào nǐ jìnlai de?
Who told you to come in?

73. Question words repeated in a complex sentence

When question words (QW) are repeated in a complex sentence, they convey ideas such as "whatever", "whoever" and "wherever".

(1) QW "哪兒 nǎr" (wherever)

73.1 你 去 哪兒， 我 就 去 哪兒。
Nǐ qù nǎr, wǒ jiù qù nǎr.
Wherever you go, I'll go with you.

73.2 哪兒 暖和， 她 去 哪兒。
Nǎr nuǎnhuo, tā qù nǎr.
She'll go wherever it is warm.

(2) QW "誰 shéi" (whoever)

73.3 誰 漂亮 我 跟 誰 結婚。
Shéi piàoliang wǒ gēn shéi jiéhūn.
I'll marry whomever is pretty.

73.4 誰 要 去 誰 去。
Shéi yào qù shéi qù.
Whoever wants to go, go.

(3) QW "甚麼 shénme" (whatever)

73.5 你 要 甚麼， 我 有 甚麼。
Nǐ yào shénme, wǒ yǒu shénme.
Whatever you want, I have it.

73.6 他們 做 甚麼， 我們 吃 甚麼。
Tāmen zuò shénme, wǒmen chī shénme.
We'll eat whatever they prepare.

(4) QW "怎麼 zěnme" (however)

73.7 鷄，她 怎麼 做 怎麼 好吃。
Jī, tā zěnme zuò zěnme hǎochī.
The chicken tastes delicious no matter how she prepares it.

73.8 爸爸 怎麼 説， 我們 怎麼 做。
Bàba zěnme shuō, wǒmen zěnme zuò.
We'll do it in whatever way Dad says.

74. Reduplication of verbs

The semantic function of reduplicating a verb is three fold:

(1) To indicate an action of short duration. The construction "Verb-le-Verb" usually indicates this function.

74.1 他 推了推 我， 叫 我 先 說。
Tā tuīletuī wǒ, jiào wǒ xiān shuō.
He pushed me and asked me to speak first.

74.2 我 看了看 她， 可是 没 跟 她 說話。
Wǒ kànlekàn tā, kěshi méi gēn tā shuōhuà.
I took a look at her, but I didn't speak to her.

(2) To make the speaker's tone less formal, that is, to soften the tone. This function is common in requests and suggestions.

74.3 讓 我 看看 你的 照片。
Ràng wǒ kànkan nǐde zhàopiàn.
Let me have a look at your photos.

74.4 請進， 請進。
Qǐngjìn, qǐngjìn.
Please do come in.

(3) To indicate things done in a casual or relaxed way. This function appears when we are listing a few actions in a complex sentence.

74.5 星期天 我 多半兒 在 家 看看 書， 聽聽 收音機， 没 甚麼 特別 事 幹。
Xīngqītian wǒ duōbànr zài jiā kànkan shū, tīngting shōuyīnjī, méi shénme tèbié shì gàn.
On Sundays I mostly read books and listen to the radio. There is nothing in particular to do.

74.6 整天 吃吃， 喝喝， 怎麼 行？
Zhěngtiān chīchi, hēhe, zěnme xíng?
Just eat and drink all day long, how can that be?

Note: When monosyllabic verbs are reduplicated, the number "一 yī" can be inserted in between (in functions (1) and (2) only). However, this practice cannot be applied to verbs of more than one syllable.

75. 人 rén and 男人 nánrén

Typical error:

He's a very learned man.
他 是 很 有 學問 的 男人。
Tā shì hěn yǒu xuéwen de nánrén.

Correct usage:

他 是 很 有 學問 的 人。
Tā shì hěn yǒu xuéwen de rén.

"人 rén" means "human being" or "man", which is used in the sense of "any human being, regardless of sex or age".

75.1 人 活着 不是 就 靠 食物。
Rén huózhe búshì jiù kào shíwù.
Man doesn't live by bread alone.

75.2 她 是 外國人。
Tā shì wàiguórén.
She is a foreigner.

75.3 他們 是 軍人。
Tāmen shì jūnrén.
They are soldiers.

"男人 nánrén" is used in the sense of "an adult male person, as distinguished from a female".

75.4 日本 女人 比 男人 長壽。
Rìběn nǚrén bǐ nánrén chángshòu.
Japanese women live longer than men.

75.5 這裏 的 男人 都 喜歡 抽煙。
Zhèli de nánrén dōu xǐhuan chōuyān.
All the men in this place like to smoke.

76. 認識 rènshi and 知道 zhīdao

Typical error:

I know his wife.
我 知道 他 太太。
Wǒ zhīdao tā tàitai.

Correct usage:

我 認識 他 太太。
Wǒ rènshi tā tàitai.

"認識 rènshi" means "to know (a person or a place)" or "to recognize". It cannot be used in the sense of "to know of" or "to know about".

76.1 你們 在 哪兒 認識 的？
Nǐmen zài nǎr rènshi de?
Where did you get to know each other?

76.2 你 認識 路 嗎？
Nǐ rènshi lù ma?
Do you know the way?

76.3 你 應該 認識 這 個 字，是不是？
Nǐ yīnggāi rènshi zhèi ge zì, shìbushì?
You should know this character, shouldn't you?

"知道 zhīdao" means "to know of" or "to know about".

76.4 我 知道 一些 關於 孔子 的 事。
Wǒ zhīdao yì xiē guānyú Kǒngzǐ de shì.
I know something about Confucius.

76.5 我 不 認識 他，可是 我 知道 他。
Wǒ bú rènshi tā, kěshi wǒ zhīdao tā.
I don't know him, but I know of him.

76.6 你 知道 怎麼 種花兒 嗎？
Nǐ zhīdao zěnme zhònghuār ma?
Do you know how to grow flowers?

77. Resultative verb compounds (RVC)

Typical errors:

Did you smell it?
你 聞 這 個 味兒 了 嗎？
Nǐ wén zhèi ge wèir le ma?

I've tried to buy that book, but I could not get it.
那 本 書， 我 買了 半天， 沒 買。
Nèi běn shū, wǒ mǎile bàntiān, méi mǎi.

Correct usage:

你 聞見 這 個 味兒 了 嗎？
Nǐ wénjian zhèi ge wèir le ma?

那 本 書， 我 買了 半天， 沒 買到。
Nèi běn shū, wǒ mǎile bàntian, méi mǎidào.

Resultative verb compounds are commonly used in both speaking and writing. They constitute one of the least understood areas of Mandarin Chinese. Hence, it is an area in which practically every student of Chinese makes a great number of mistakes. A clear understanding of the resultative verb compound is, therefore, essential to learning Chinese.

Resultative verbs are compounds of two elements, in which the first element shows the kind of action involved, while the second indicates the result or extent of the first element.

The distinction between action verbs and the resultative verbs may help us to better understand the latter.

Compare:

77.1 那 本 書， 他 買了。
Nèi běn shū, tā mǎile.
He bought that book.

77.2 那 本 書， 他 買到了。
Nèi běn shū, tā mǎidàole.
He managed to buy that book.

In ⟨77.1⟩ we are concerned with what he did, whereas in ⟨77.2⟩ we are not con-

concerned with the action "買 mǎi" (buy), but rather with the result "He finally managed to get a copy of that book". Resultative verbs emphasize the result of an action. Note the following three points:

(1) The Resultative verb compound is formed in this way:

Verb { monosyllabic / disyllabic } + Result { monosyllabic / disyllabic } = Resultative verb compound

(2) There are many commonly used resultative verb endings (i.e. the second element of a RVC) which can be shared by a group of verbs.

Examples:

V + 破 pò (break or hurt)

打破 dǎpò	hit and break
摔破 shuāipò	fall and hurt
寫破 xiěpò	write and poke through
穿破 chuānpò	wear out

V + 去 qù (go)

上去 shàngqu	go up
下去 xiàqu	go down
進去 jìnqu	go in
出去 chūqu	go out

V + 到 dào (arrive or succeed)

拿到 nádào	bring/take to
想到 xiǎngdào	think of
說到 shuōdào	speak of/ say up to
碰到 pèngdào	meet

(3) With a given action, there is a given result. When the result is achievable, we insert "得 dé" between the action and the result. If the result is unachievable, we insert "不 bù" instead.

77.3 他 把 鞋 穿破 了。
Tā bǎ xié chuānpò le.
His shoes are worn out.

77.4 那 本 書，我 買不到。
Nèi běn shū, wǒ mǎibudào.
I'm unable to get that book.

77.5 你 寫得完 這 些 字 嗎？
Nǐ xiědewán zhèi xiē zì ma?
Can you finish writing these characters?

77.6 我 買不起 "奔馳"牌 轎車。
Wǒ mǎibuqǐ "Bēnchí"pái jiàochē.
I can't afford to buy a "Mercedes Benz".

78. 上算 shàngsuàn

Typical error:

This is a good bargain.
這 是 很 好的 上算。
Zhèi shì hěn hǎode shàngsuàn.

Correct usage:

這 個 很 上算。
Zhèi ge hěn shàngsuàn.

"上算 shàngsuàn" means "be a bargain", "worth it", "get one's money's worth". It is an adjective, not a noun.

78.1 買 來回票 上算。
Mǎi láihuípiào shàngsuàn.
It's cheaper to buy a round-trip ticket.

78.2 在 香港 買 東西 上算。
Zài Xiānggǎng mǎi dōngxi shàngsuàn.
When you are shopping in Hong Kong, you get your money's worth.

79. 是……的 shì ... de construction for past events

The "是……的 shì ... de" construction is used when we are focusing on the *different circumstances* under which some actions took place. These circumstances include time, place, purpose, price, means of action, and agent or receiver of an action.

Note the following four points:

(1) The equative verb "是 shì" in this construction may be omitted in spoken Chinese.

(2) The construction always includes a verb and some adverbial expression (time, place, purpose, etc.) that precedes it.

(3) When the verb takes an object, the object is either placed before or after "的 de". If the object happens to be a pronoun, it is normally placed before "的 de".

(4) When we use the construction in the negative form, "不 bù" is placed before "是……的 shì ... de".

Time

79.1 他 不是 昨天 告訴 我 的。
Tā búshì zuótian gàosu wǒ de.
It wasn't yesterday that he told me about it.

Place

79.2 我 是 北京 大學 畢的業。
Wǒ shì Běijīng Dàxué bìdeyè.
I graduated from Beijing University.

Purpose

79.3 我們 是 來 學 漢語 的。
Wǒmen shì lái xué Hànyǔ de.
We came to study Chinese.

Price

79.4 那 本 書 是 一百 塊 買 的。
Nèi běn shū shì yìbǎi kuài mǎi de.
That book cost one hundred dollars./ It cost one hundred dollars to buy that book.

Means of Action

79.5 他們 是 坐 飛機 來 的。
Tāmen shì zuò fēijī lái de.
They came by airplane.

Agent of an Action

79.6 這 些 糖 是 她 買 的。
Zhèi xiē táng shì tā mǎi de.
She bought this candy./ It was she who bought this candy.

Receiver of an Action

79.7 我 是 吃的 西餐， 不是 吃的 中餐。
Wǒ shì chīde Xīcān, búshì chīde Zhōngcān.
I had Western food, not Chinese food.

80. 是……的 shì ... de and 了 le

Typical errors:

We learned it little by little.
我們 學了 一點兒 一點兒。
Wǒmen xuéle yìdiǎnr yìdiǎnr.

When did he graduate?
他 甚麼 時候 畢業了？
Tā shénme shíhou bìyèle?

Correct usage:

我們 是 一點兒 一點兒 學的。
Wǒmen shì yìdiǎnr yìdiǎnr xuéde.

他 甚麼 時候 畢的業？
Tā shénme shíhou bìdeyè?

There is one fundamental difference between the "是……的 shì ... de" construction (past events) and "了 le". With "是……的 shì ... de" construction, our focus is on the *circumstances* of action, not on the action itself, whereas with "了 le" our focus is on the *action*, that is, whether the action is completed or not.

Compare:

80.1 她 是 昨天 來 的。
Tā shì zuótian lái de.
She came *yesterday*.

80.2 她 昨天 來了。
Tā zuótian láile.
She *came* yesterday.

With 〈80.1〉 we are concerned with "when she came" instead of "whether she came or not", whereas with 〈80.2〉 we are interested in knowing "whether she came or not". The distinction here can be clearly seen when these two sentences are changed into the question form.

80.3 她 是 甚麼 時候 來 的？
Tā shì shénme shíhou lái de?
When did she come?

80.4 她　昨天　來了 嗎？
Tā zuótian láile ma?
Did she come yesterday?

Now let us take the first of the typical errors listed above as another example. The sentence "我們學了一點一點 Wǒmen xuéle yìdiǎn yìdiǎn" is incorrect since the speaker's focus is on the circumstances of the action "學 xué" (i.e. the manner in which they learned it). The speaker does *not* focus on the action with an indefinite quantifier, which would have been "我們學了一點兒 Wǒmen xuéle yìdiǎnr", meaning "We learned a little bit". Hence this sentence should be "我們是一點一點地學的 Wǒmen shì yìdiǎn yìdiǎn de xué de" which means "We learned it little by little".

81. 試試 shìshi and 想要 xiǎng yào

Typical error:

He tried to hit me.
他　試試　打　我。
Tā　shìshi　dǎ　wǒ.

Correct usage:

他　想　要　打　我。
Tā　xiǎng　yào　dǎ　wǒ.

" 試試 shìshi" means "to try, taste, sample, test".

81.1 請　試試　這　個　湯。
Qǐng　shìshi　zhèi　ge　tāng.
Please try this soup.

81.2 他　要　試試　這　輛　車　的　快慢。
Tā　yào　shìshi　zhèi　liàng　chē　de　kuàimàn.
He wants to test the speed of this car.

81.3 你　試試　這　件　襯衫　合適　不　合適。
Nǐ　shìshi　zhèi　jiàn　chènshān　héshì　bù　héshì.
Try this shirt on and see if it fits.

81.4 讓　我　試試　說服　她。
Ràng　wǒ　shìshi　shuōfú　tā.
Let me try and convince her.

We use " 想要 xiǎng yào/ 想 xiǎng" (informal) or " 試圖 shìtú (formal)/ 企圖 qìtú (used mainly in a derogatory sense)" in the sense of "try to" or "attempt". The difference between " 試試 shìshi" and " 想 要 xiǎng yào" is that " 想 要 xiǎng yào" normally implies "a failed attempt".

81.5 他　想　要　打　電話　給　我，可是　没　打通。
Tā　xiǎng　yào　dǎ　diànhuà　gěi　wǒ,　kěshi　méi　dǎtōng.
He tried to call me, but he couldn't get through.

81.6 你　想　要　說　甚麼？試試　慢慢兒　說。
Nǐ　xiǎng　yào　shuō　shénme?　Shìshi　mànmānr　shuō.
What are you trying to say? Try to say it slowly.

81.7 她　想　要　騙　我。
Tā xiǎng yào piàn wǒ.
She tried to fool me.

Note: " 想 要 xiǎng yào" can also be used in the sense of "intend to" or "would like to".

81.8 你　想　要　買　甚麼？
Nǐ xiǎng yào mǎi shénme?
What would you like to buy?

82. 收 shōu and 收到 shōudào

Typical error:

She received a letter today.
她 今天 收了 一 封 信。
Tā jīntian shōule yì fēng xìn.

Correct usage:

她 今天 收到 了 一 封 信。
Tā jīntiān shōudào le yì fēng xìn.

"收 shōu" means "accept", "take", "collect". The sentence "她今天收了一封信 Tā jīntian shōule yì fēng xìn" would be correct if "收 shōu" were used in the sense of "collect", not in the sense of "receive".

82.1 別 收 他的 禮物。
Bié shōu tāde lǐwù.
Don't accept his gift.

82.2 今天 收信了 嗎？
Jīntian shōuxìnle ma?
Have the letters been collected today?

"收到 shōudào" is a resultative verb. It means "receive".

82.3 我們 收到 了 她的 電報。
Wǒmen shōudào le tāde diànbào.
We have received her telegram.

82.4 我 一 收到 好 消息 就 告訴 大家。
Wǒ yì shōudào hǎo xiāoxi jiù gàosu dàjiā.
As soon as I receive the good news, I'll let everybody know.

83. 摔 shuāi and 掉 diào

(1) When we want to say a person "falls off" a high place or "falls into" a river, either "摔 shuāi" or "掉 diào" can be used.

83.1 他 掉在 河裏 了。/他 摔到 河裏 去了。
Tā diàozai héli le./Tā shuāidào héli qùle.
He fell into the river.

83.2 那 個 孩子 從 樹 上 摔/掉下來 了。
Nèi ge háizi cóng shù shang shuāi/diàoxialai le.
That child fell out of a tree.

(2) When we talk about the fall of an object onto the ground or floor, "掉 diào" is used to mean either "fall" (by itself) or "drop" (by a person) while "摔 shuāi" is used to indicate "throw".

83.3 別 掉在 地上。
Bié diàozai dìshang.
Don't drop it on the floor.

83.4 他的 筆 掉在 地上 了。
Tāde bǐ diàozai dìshang le.
His pen fell on the floor.

Note: Unlike the English usage, in Chinese we tend to use the passive form. In other words, instead of saying "I dropped my pen on the floor" we say "My pen fell on the floor".

83.5 老師 把 粉筆 摔在 地上 了。
Lǎoshī bǎ fěnbǐ shuàizai dìshang le.
The teacher threw his chalk on the floor.

(3) "摔 shuāi" can be used to mean "fall and break", whereas "掉 diào" can only mean "fall".

83.6 我 摔了 我的 杯子。
Wǒ shuāile wǒde bēizi.
I broke my glass.

83.7 我的 杯子 掉在 地上 了。
Wǒde bēizi diàozai dìshang le.
My glass fell on the floor.

(4) "摔 shuāi" can be used in the sense of "stumble" or "trip", whereas "掉 diào" cannot. However, when "摔 shuāi" is used in this sense, it normally takes a resultative verb ending.

83.8 那 位 老 太太 摔倒了， 可是 没 摔着。
Nèi wèi lǎo tàitai shuāidǎole, kěshi méi shuāizháo.
That old lady stumbled, but didn't get hurt.

84. 睡覺 shuìjiào and 睡着 shuìzháo

(1) "睡覺 shuìjiào" is a verb-object compound, whereas "睡着 shuìzháo" is a resultative verb compound.
(2) "睡覺 shùijiào" is normally used in the sense of "go to bed", though occasionally it can be interpreted as "sleep". "睡着 shuìzháo" is only used in the sense of "sleep".

84.1 你　平常　幾　點　鐘　睡覺？
Nǐ píngcháng jǐ diǎn zhōng shuìjiào?
Generally what time do you go to bed?

84.2 他　一　躺下　就　睡着了。
Tā yì tǎngxia jiù shuìzháole.
As soon as he lies down, he's asleep (he falls asleep).

84.3 北方人　睡　午覺　嗎？
Běifāngrén shuì wǔjiào ma?
Do Northerners take a nap after lunch?

84.4 我　是　十　點　鐘　睡的覺，十一　點　多　才　睡着　的。
Wǒ shì shí diǎn zhōng shuìdejiào, shíyī diǎn duō cái shuìzháo de.
I went to bed at ten o'clock, but it wasn't until after eleven that I fell asleep.

85. 送 sòng and 帶 dài

"送 sòng" is used in the sense of "to see someone off". It is also used in a situation in which one accompanies or takes another person to a place (e.g. home, airport, etc.) with the intention of keeping him company or giving him a ride.

85.1 我 明天 到 機場 去 送 你。
Wǒ míngtian dào jīchǎng qù sòng nǐ.
I'll see you off at the airport tomorrow.

85.2 請 你 送 她 到 機場 去，好 嗎？
Qǐng nǐ sòng tā dào jīchǎng qù, hǎo ma?
Would you please take her to the airport?

85.3 誰 送 你 回家？
Shéi sòng nǐ huíjiā?
Who's going to take you home?

"帶 dài" is used in the sense of "to lead someone to a place" or "to accompany someone to a place in order to show him the way or show him around". It can also be used in a situation in which one takes another person to a place for some activity (e.g. a party, football game, etc.).

85.4 請 你 帶路，好 嗎？
Qǐng nǐ dàilù, hǎo ma?
Would you please lead the way?

85.5 請 你 帶 她 到 機場 去 看看，好 嗎？
Qǐng nǐ dài tā dào jīchǎng qù kànkan, hǎo ma?
Would you please take her to the airport and show her around?

85.6 請 你 一定 得 帶 你 太太 跟 孩子 一塊兒 來。
Qǐng nǐ yídìng děi dài nǐ tàitai gēn háizi yíkuàr lái.
Please do bring your wife and children along.

86. 算 suàn, 算了 suànle, 算上 suànshang, etc.

"算 suàn" means "to calculate" or "to figure". It also means "to consider" or "to regard as".

86.1 你 算算 這 個 月 我們 一共 花了 多少 錢。
Nǐ suànsuan zhèi ge yuè wǒmen yígòng huāle duōshǎo qián.
Calculate the total amount of money that we spent this month.

86.2 她 算了算, 這 次 旅行 得 要 五千 塊 錢。
Tā suànlesuàn, zhèi cì lǚxíng děi yào wǔqiān kuài qián.
She figured that this trip would cost five thousand dollars.

86.3 這 個 地方 不 算 熱鬧。
Zhèi ge dìfang bú suàn rènao.
This place is not considered a hectic place.

"算了 suànle" is an idiom which means "it's all right" or "forget it".

86.4 要是 天氣 不 好 就 算了。
Yàoshi tiānqi bù hǎo jiù suànle.
If the weather is no good then forget it.

86.5 算了, (要是) 你 不 願 去 就 別 去。
Suànle, (yàoshi) nǐ bú yuàn qù jiù bié qù.
Forget it! If you don't want to go, don't go.

"算上 suànshang" means "to count in", "to include".

86.6 別 把 我 算上。
Bié bǎ wǒ suànshang.
Don't count me in.

86.7 算上 你們, 我們 一共 有 十 個 人。
Suànshang nǐmen, wǒmen yígòng yǒu shí ge rén.
Including you, altogether there are ten of us.

"算出來 suànchulai" is a resultative verb compound, which means "to figure out".

86.8 我們 花了 多少 錢, 你 算出來 了 嗎?
Wǒmen huāle duōshǎo qián, nǐ suànchulai le ma?
Have you figured out how much money we've spent?

86.9 你 算得出來 她 該 找 你 多少 錢 嗎?
Nǐ suàndechūlái tā gāi zhǎo nǐ duōshǎo qián ma?
Can you figure out how much change she should give you?

"算完 suànwán" means "to finish counting or calculating".

86.10 我 算得出來 他們的 人數， 可是 五分 鐘 以內
Wǒ suàndechūlái tāmende rénshù, kěshi wǔfēn zhōng yǐnèi
算不完。
suànbuwán.
I can figure out the number of their people, but I can't have it done (figured) in five minutes' time.

86.11 我 已經 算完了 口算。
Wǒ yǐjing suànwánle kǒusuàn.
I've finished the oral calculation.

87. Verbs and verb-object compounds

Typical errors:

He likes to drink.
他　喜歡　喝。
Tā xǐhuan hē.

I write Chinese characters.
我　寫字　中國字。
Wǒ xiězì Zhōngguózì.

Correct usage:

他　喜歡　喝酒。
Tā xǐhuan hējiǔ.

我　寫　中國字。
Wǒ xiě Zhōngguózì.

Students of Chinese frequently come across transitive verbs with general objects, which are not used in English.

Note these three points:

(1) Unless it is already known to the listener, the general object of a verb-object compound *cannot* be omitted. If it were left out, then the speaker would be making himself unintelligible. For example, when an English speaker says "I love to drink ", the listener would automatically understand the drink to be "any alcoholic beverage", even though the general object "alcoholic beverage" is not used. This is not so in Chinese. If one says "我愛喝 wǒ ài hē" the listener would not know what the speaker loves to drink. Hence, the general object "酒 jiǔ" (alcoholic beverage) is required in order to make the sentence intelligible.

87.1 他　喜歡　唱歌。
Tā xǐhuan chànggē.
He likes to sing.

87.2 她　每天　看書。
Tā měitian kànshū.
She reads everyday.

87.3 這　個　孩子　真　愛　打架。
Zhèi ge háizi zhēn ài dǎjià.
This child really loves to fight.

(2) Since the verb-object compound already has an object, it cannot take another one after it. However, if a specific object is required, then the general object should be replaced by the specific one.

87.4 我 會 做 法國菜。
Wǒ huì zuò Fǎguocài.
I can make French food.

87.5 他 喜歡 喝 啤酒。
Tā xǐhuan hē píjiǔ.
He likes to drink beer.

87.6 她 每天 看 小說。
Tā měitian kàn xiǎoshuō.
She reads novels everyday.

(3) The two elements of a verb-object compound may be separated by the verb suffix "了 le", a measure word or another modifier.

87.7 我 寫了 三 封 信。
Wǒ xiěle sān fēng xìn.
I wrote three letters.

87.8 你 洗 (一) 個 熱水 澡 吧。
Nǐ xǐ (yí) ge rèshuǐ zǎo ba.
Won't you take a hot bath?

87.9 別 睡 懶覺！
Bié shuì lǎnjiào!
Don't get up late!

88. 爲 wèi, 給 gěi, 替 tì

"爲 wèi" has two meanings:

(1) It is used in the sense of "for the benefit of" and is often rendered as "for" in English. Its grammatical function is to introduce the object of an action. It is equivalent to "給 gěi" or "替 tì".

88.1 他 爲/給 我 買了 一 台 電視機。
Tā wèi/gěi wǒ mǎile yì tái diànshìjī.
He bought me a TV set.

88.2 媽媽 爲/給/替 妹妹 做了 一 件 裙子。
Māma wèi/gěi/tì mèimei zuòle yí jiàn qúnzi.
Mother has made a skirt for little sister.

(2) It means "for the purpose of" and introduces the aim or reason for an action. It may take either "了 le" or "着 zhe" directly after it.

88.3 爲 現代化 努力 工作。
Wèi xiàndàihuà nǔlì gōngzuò.
Work hard for the modernization (program).

88.4 他 學習 漢語 是 爲了 和 中國 做 貿易。
Tā xuéxí Hànyǔ shì wèile hé Zhōngguó zuò màoyì.
He studies Chinese in order to do trade with China.

When "給 gěi" is used as a coverb, it has three primary meanings:

(1) It means "to" and always introduces an animate indirect object.

88.5 她 給 父母 寫了 一 封 信。
Tā gěi fùmǔ xiěle yì fēng xìn.
She wrote a letter to her parents.

88.6 昨天 我 給 姐姐 打了 一 封 電報。
Zuótian wǒ gěi jiějie dǎle yì fēng diànbào.
I sent a telegram to my sister yesterday.

(2) It means "for" and introduces a person for whom a service is done. It is equivalent to "爲 wèi" or "替 tì".

88.7 去 給/替 他 找 一下 書包。
Qù gěi/tì tā zhǎo yíxià shūbāo.
Go find his school bag for him.

88.8 醫生 給/替 我 檢查 身體。
Yīshēng gěi/tì wǒ jiǎnchá shēntǐ.
The doctor gives me a medical check-up.

(3) It is used for passive constructions, and functions like "被 bèi", another passive marker.

88.9 我 給 他 打了 一 頓。
Wǒ gěi tā dǎle yí dùn.
I was beaten up by him.

88.10 門 給 風 吹壞了。
Mén gěi fēng chuīhuàile.
The door was damaged by the wind.

See also "給 gěi" as a post verb at entry 31.

"替 tì" has two meanings:

(1) It means "in place of".

88.11 誰 能 替 我 教書？
Shéi néng tì wǒ jiāoshū?
Who can teach in my place?

88.12 你 可以 替 他 去 比賽 嗎？
Nǐ kěyǐ tì tā qù bǐsài ma?
Can you go and replace him in the contest?

(2) It means "for" and is equivalent to "爲 wèi" or "給 gěi".

88.13 我們 大家 都 替/爲 你 高興。
Wǒmen dàjiā dōu tì/wèi nǐ gāoxìng.
All of us feel happy for you.

88.14 你 能 替/給/爲 我 做 件 事 嗎？
Nǐ néng tì/gěi/wèi wǒ zuò jiàn shì ma?
Can you do me a favor?

88.15 你 也 能 替/給 我 畫 張 畫兒 嗎？
Nǐ yě néng tì/gěi wǒ huà zhāng huàr ma?
Can you paint me a picture too?

89. 想起來 xiǎngqilai and 想出來 xiǎngchulai

Typical error:

I can't come up with a way./I can't figure out a way.
我 想不起來 一 個 法子。
Wǒ xiǎngbùqǐlái yí ge fázi.

Correct usage:

我 想不出來 一 個 法子。
Wǒ xiǎngbùchūlái yí ge fázi.

"想起來 xiǎngqilai" is a resultative verb and it means "remember" or "recall".

89.1 她 看着 相片 就 想起 老家 來了。
Tā kànzhe xiàngpiàn jiù xiǎngqǐ lǎojiā laile.
While looking at the photo, she recalled her old home.

89.2 我 想起 她的 名字 來了。
Wǒ xiǎngqǐ tāde míngzi laile.
Now I remember her name.

Note: Unless it is used in the potential form as in 〈89.3〉 and 〈89.4〉, the resultative verb complement "來 lái" is normally placed after a noun.

89.3 你 想得起來 那 本 書 的 作者 嗎？
Nǐ xiǎngdeqǐlái nèi běn shū de zuòzhě ma?
Are you able to recall the author of that book?

89.4 他 想不起來 是 在 哪兒 見到 她 的。
Tā xiǎngbuqǐlái shì zài nǎr jiàndào tā de.
He can't recall where he met her before.

Note: the basic distinction between "想起來 xiǎngqilai" and "記得 jìde" is that the former can be used in the positive potential form of the resultative verb (i.e. "想得起來 xiǎngdeqǐlái" [able to recall]), whereas the latter cannot. Hence, questions which begin with "Are you able to recall ...?" would use "想得起來 xiǎngdeqǐlái", and those with "Do you remember ...?" "記得 jìde".

89.5 你 還 記得 我的 名字 嗎？
Nǐ hái jìde wǒde míngzi ma?
Do you still remember my name?

"想出來 xiǎngchulai" means "to figure out" or "to come up with". We often use it to talk about "figuring out a way", "coming up with a plan, a reply, design, etc."

89.6 我 想出來 一 個 好 主意。
Wǒ xiǎngchulai yí ge hǎo zhúyi.
I've come up with a good idea./ I've thought of a good idea.

89.7 最後 她 想出來 一 個 解決 的 辦法。
Zuìhòu tā xiǎngchulai yí ge jiějué de bànfǎ.
Finally, she came up with a solution.

89.8 學生 的 中國 名字，我 還 没 想出來 呢。
Xuésheng de Zhōngguó míngzi, wǒ hái méi xiǎngchulai ne.
I have not yet come up with Chinese names for the students.

90. 些 xiē

"些 xiē" is measure word, which indicates an unspecified quantity (or degree), normally a small one. When it is used after the specifiers "這 zhèi" and "那 nèi", it functions as a plural marker.

90.1 她 買了 些 菜 就 回家了。
Tā mǎile xiē cài jiù huíjiāle.
She bought some food and then went home.

90.2 有 些 人 喜歡 很 早 起來 跑步。
Yǒu xiē rén xǐhuan hěn zǎo qǐlai pǎobù.
Some people like to get up early and go jogging.

90.3 這 些 橘子 酸不酸？
Zhèi xiē júzi suānbusuān?
Are these oranges sour?

90.4 我 比 他 胖 一 些。
Wǒ bǐ tā pàng yì xiē.
I'm a little fatter than he.

91. 學 xué and 學會 xuéhuì

Typical error:

He studied Chinese for one year, but failed to learn it.
中文 他 學了 一 年，可是 没 學。
Zhōngwén tā xuéle yì nián, kěshi méi xué.

Correct usage:

中文 他 學了 一 年，可是 没 學會。
Zhōngwén tā xuéle yì nián, kěshì méi xuéhuì.

The distinction between "學 xué" and "學會 xuéhuì" is that the former refers to the act of acquiring knowledge whereas the latter refers to the positive result of that act. Hence, "學 xué" means "study" or "learn" whereas "學會 xuéhuì" means "succeed in learning".

91.1 你們 的 功課 學會 了 嗎？
Nǐmen de gōngkè xuéhuì le ma?
Have you learned your lessons?

91.2 你 是 在 哪兒 學會 用 筷子 的？
Nǐ shì zài nǎr xuéhuì yòng kuàizi de?
Where did you learn how to use chopsticks?

91.3 你 既然 已經 開始 學 開車了，就 得 把 它 學會。
Nǐ jìrán yǐjing kāishǐ xué kāichēle, jiù děi bǎ tā xuéhuì.
Since you've already started to learn to drive, you must finish and be able to drive.

92. 要 yào

This one-syllable modal verb is used in many spoken situations. It is essential to learn the following four usages of "要 yào":

(1) It means "want".

92.1 我 要 一 輛 自行車。
Wǒ yào yí liàng zìxíngchē.
I want a bicycle.

92.2 誰 要 去 買 東西 去?
Shéi yào qù mǎi dōngxi qu?
Who wants to go shopping?

(2) It means "should", "need".

92.3 你 要 多 喝 開水, 多 休息。
Nǐ yào duō hē kāishuǐ, duō xiūxi.
You should drink a lot of water and get more rest.

92.4 水果 要 先 洗洗 再 吃。
Shuǐguǒ yào xiān xǐxi zài chī.
You should (first) wash the fruit before eating it.

(3) It means "don't" when it is used in the idiom "不要 búyào".

92.5 請 安靜, 不要 說話。
Qǐng ānjìng, búyào shuōhuà.
Please be quiet. Don't talk.

92.6 不要 再 喝了, 你 都 快 醉了。
Búyào zài hēle, nǐ dōu kuài zuìle.
Don't drink any more. You're getting drunk already.

(4) It means "will" or "going to" (positive sentences only).

92.7 他們 明天 要 到 中國 去。
Tāmen míngtian yào dào Zhōngguó qù.
They're going to China tomorrow.

92.8 她 要 送 一 本 字典 給 我。
Tā yào sòng yì běn zìdiǎn gěi wǒ.
She's going to give me a dictionary.

92.9 他 要 下月 底 才 能 回來。
Tā yào xiàyuè dǐ cái néng huílai.
He won't be able to return until the end of next month.

92.10 看 樣子 他們 要 結婚。
Kàn yàngzi tāmen yào jiéhūn.
It looks as if they will get married.

93. 要是……就 yàoshi ... jiù

Typical error:

If I were you, I would go.
要是 我 是 你，就 我 去。
Yàoshì wǒ shì nǐ, jiù wǒ qù.

Correct usage:

要是 我 是 你，我 就 去。
Yàoshì wǒ shì nǐ, wǒ jiù qù.

We use the pattern "要是……就 yàoshi ... jiù" for conditional situations.

Note: If we use a pronoun or noun in the second part of the pattern, we should place it *before* "就 jiù", not *after* it.

93.1 你 要是 不 喜歡 他，就 別 理 他。
Nǐ yàoshì bù xǐhuan tā, jiù bié lǐ tā.
If you don't like him, don't pay any attention to him.

93.2 要是 我 有 錢，我 就 到 英國 去 旅行。
Yàoshi wǒ yǒu qián, wǒ jiù dào Yīngguó qù lǚxíng.
If I had money, I would go to England to travel.

93.3 要是 你 來了，問題 就 解決了。
Yàoshi nǐ láile, wèntí jiù jiějuéle.
Had you come, the problem would have been solved.

94. 一……就 yī ... jiù

Typical error:

Did you leave as soon as the school closed for vacation?
你 一 離開 就 學校 放假了 嗎？
Nǐ yì líkāi jiù xuéxiào fàngjiàle ma?

Correct usage:

學校 一 放假， 你 就 離開/走 了 嗎？
Xuéxiào yí fàngjià, nǐ jiù líkāi/zǒu le ma?

The pattern "一……就 yī ... jiù" means "as soon as". We use it to connect two events, one taking place immediately after the other. Note that if both events or actions are habitual, then the pattern conveys the idea of "whenever".

94.1 他 一 來， 我 就 走。
Tā yì lái, wǒ jiù zǒu.
I'll leave as soon as he comes.

94.2 她 一 放學 就 回家了。
Tā yí fàngxué jiù huíjiāle.
She went home as soon as classes were over.

94.3 我 一 高興 就 喝酒。
Wǒ yì gāoxìng jiù hējiǔ.
I'll drink whenever I feel happy.

Note the structural distinction between the Chinese and English sentences.

95. 一……也 yī ... yě

The pattern "一……也 yī ... yě" is used when we want to say "not even one" or "not at all". It is only used in a negative sense. Hence, either "不 bù" or "没 méi" is used after "也 yě".

95.1 他 一分 錢 也 没有。
Tā yìfēn qián yě méiyǒu.
He is penniless.

95.2 她 寫字， 一 個 也 没 寫錯。
Tā xiězì, yí ge yě méi xiěcuò.
She didn't make a single mistake in her character writing.

95.3 這 本 書 一點兒 也 不 貴。
Zhèi běn shū yìdiǎnr yě bú guì.
This book is not at all expensive.

95.4 我 中國 一 次 也 没 去過。
Wǒ Zhōngguó yí cì yě méi qùguo.
I've not even once been to China.

95.5 她 一點兒 也 不 喜歡 你。
Tā yìdiǎnr yě bù xǐhuan nǐ.
She doesn't like you a bit.

96. 一點兒 yìdiǎnr

"一點兒 yìdiǎnr" is used when we want to talk about small quantities or degrees. It is used either adverbially, before or after a verb or adjective, or attributively, before a noun.

96.1 請 你 晚上 早 (一) 點兒 來。
Qǐng nǐ wǎnshang zǎo (yì) diǎnr lái.
Please come a little earlier tonight.

96.2 我 想 買 (一) 點兒 菜。
Wǒ xiǎng mǎi (yì) diǎnr cài.
I want to buy a bit of food.

96.3 今天 熱了 (一) 點兒。
Jīntian rèle (yì) diǎnr.
It's a little hotter today.

96.4 這 個 顏色 深了 (一) 點兒。
Zhèi ge yánsè shēnle (yì) diǎnr.
This color is a bit darker.

Note: In speech, the numerical "一 yī" is often omitted.

97. 一定 yídìng and 一定得 yídìng děi

Typical error:

You must go.
你　一定　去！
Nǐ　yídìng　qù!

Correct usage:

你　一定　得　去！
Nǐ　yídìng　děi　qù!

"一定 yídìng" means "certainly". We normally use it in declarative sentences. However, if and when "一定 yídìng" is used in an imperative sentence, it is then interchangeable with "一定 得 yídìng děi".

97.1 **A:** 你　今天　晚上　一定／一定　得　來　啊！
Nǐ　jīntian　wǎnshang　yídìng / yídìng　děi　lái　ya!
You must come tonight.

B: 一定　來。
Yídìng　lái.
Definitely / I'll definitely come.

97.2 他　明天　一定　不　來　上課。
Tā　míngtian　yídìng　bù　lái　shàngkè.
He's definitely not coming to class tomorrow.

97.3 你　一定　弄錯　了。
Nǐ　yídìng　nòngcuò　le.
You must be mistaken.

97.4 我　一定　得　把　字　學好。
Wǒ　yídìng　děi　bǎ　zì　xuéhǎo.
I must study the characters well.

97.5 她　先生　一定　得　多　休息。
Tā　xiānsheng　yídìng　děi　duō　xiūxi.
Her husband must take more rest.

97.6 你　一定　得　坐車　去。
Nǐ　yídìng　děi　zuòchē　qù.
You must go there by car.

Notes: (1) We may use "一定 要 yídìng yào" interchangeably with "一定 得 yídìng děi".
(2) The negative form of "一定 得 yídìng děi" (i.e. "mustn't" or "by no means") is "千萬 別 qiānwàn bié" or "一定 不要 yídìng búyào".

97.7 你 千萬 別 來 晚。
Nǐ qiānwàn bié lái wǎn.
You mustn't be late.

97.8 他 一定 不要 不 上課。
Tā yídìng búyào bú shàngkè.
He mustn't miss class.

97.9 你們 千萬 別 忘了 明天 是 她的 生日。
Nǐmen qiānwàn bié wàngle míngtian shì tāde shēngrì.
You mustn't forget tomorrow is her birthday.

98. 以前 yǐqián and 以後 yǐhòu

Typical error:

Before I eat, I first wash my hands.
以前 吃飯， 我 先 洗手。
Yǐqián chīfàn, wǒ xiān xǐshǒu.

Correct usage:

吃飯 以前， 我 先 洗手。
Chīfàn yǐqián, wǒ xiān xǐshǒu.

"以前 yǐqián" is used as either a time word or a location noun. We use it to indicate a period of time which is earlier than the present time or any given period of time. It is used in three ways:

(1) As a noun, it means "in the past" or "former". As a time word, it appears before the verb in a sentence.

98.1 以前 我 教書。
Yǐqián wǒ jiaōshū.
I taught in the past.

98.2 這 位 是 我 以前的 同事。
Zhèi wèi shì wǒ yǐqiánde tóngshì.
This is my former colleague.

(2) It is used after a "time-spent" expression (e.g. for three days). Its meaning is "ago".

98.3 三 天 以前， 他 丟了 一 把 雨傘。
Sān tiān yǐqián, tā diūle yì bǎ yǔsǎn.
He lost an umbrella three days ago.

98.4 很久 很久 以前， 有 一 位 美麗的 公主。
Hěnjiǔ hěnjiǔ yǐqián, yǒu yí wèi měilìde gōngzhǔ.
Long, long ago, there lived a beautiful princess.

(3) It is used after a "time-when" expression (e.g. at ten o'clock) or after a verb. Its meaning is "before".

98.5 她 是 國慶 以前 到 的 北京。
Tā shì Guóqìng yǐqián dào de Běijīng.
She arrived in Beijing before the National Day.

98.6 他 睡覺 以前 常常 聽 音樂。
Tā shuìjiào yǐqián chángcháng tīng yīnyuè.
He often listens to music before he goes to sleep.

"以後 yǐhòu" can also be used as a time word or a location noun. We use it to indicate a period of time which is later than the present time or any given period of time. It is used in three ways:

(1) As a time word, it means "afterwards", "later", or "in the future". It is used before the verb in a sentence.

98.7 以後 你 別 再 遲到了。
Yǐhòu nǐ bié zài chídàole.
Don't be late in the future.

98.8 他 以後 怎麼了，我 不 知道。
Tā yǐhòu zěnmele, wǒ bù zhīdao.
I don't know what happened to him afterwards.

(2) It is used after a "time-spent" expression. Its meaning is "later" or "in X's time".

98.9 三 天 以後，我 就 從 宿舍 搬出來了。
Sān tiān yǐhòu, wǒ jiù cóng sùshè bānchulaile.
I moved out from the dormitory three days later.

98.10 三 天 以後，我 就 在 中國 了。
Sān tiān yǐhòu, wǒ jiù zài Zhōngguó le.
In three days' time I'll be in China.

(3) It is used after a "time-when" expression or a verb. Its meaning is "after".

98.11 晚上 十 點 以後，商店 就 都 關門 了。
Wǎnshang shí diǎn yǐhòu, shāngdiàn jiù dōu guānmén le.
The shops will all be closed after 10:00 p.m.

98.12 做完 功課 以後，你 上 哪兒 去？
Zuòwán gōngkè yǐhòu, nǐ shàng nǎr qù?
Where will you go after your homework is done?

99. 用功 yònggōng and 努力 nǔlì

"用功 yònggōng" means "hardworking" or "work hard". We use it only when we are talking about studies.

99.1 你 得 用功 讀書。
Nǐ děi yònggōng dúshū.
You must work hard at your studies.

99.2 要 考試 了，所以 他 很 用功。
Yào kǎoshì le, suǒyǐ tā hěn yònggōng.
The exams are coming so he is working very hard.

"努力 nǔlì" means "make great effort" or "try hard". We can use it to talk about studies and any other kind of work. It can also be used as a noun.

99.3 要 學好 漢語， 你 得 盡 最 大 努力。
Yào xuéhǎo Hànyǔ, nǐ děi jìn zuì dà nǔlì.
You must do the best you can in order to master Chinese.

99.4 台灣 努力 發展 經濟。
Táiwān nǔlì fāzhǎn jīngjì.
Taiwan strives to develop its economy.

100. 有的 yǒude and 一些 yìxiē

Typical error:

I gave my younger sister some books.
我 給了 我 妹妹 有的 書。
Wǒ gěile wǒ mèimei yǒude shū.

Correct usage:

我 給了 我 妹妹 一些 書。
Wǒ gěile wǒ mèimei yìxiē shū.

(1) Both "有的 yǒude" and "一些 yìxiē" are rendered as "some" in English.
(2) "一些 yìxiē" may be used after the verb in a sentence, whereas "有的 yǒude" may not.
(3) When "一些 yìxiē" is used directly after a verb, the numerical "一 yī" is normally omitted.

100.1 我 有 一些 問題 問 你。
Wǒ yǒu yìxiē wèntí wèn nǐ.
I have some questions to ask you.

100.2 她 喝了 些 粥 就 上班 去了。
Tā hēle xiē zhōu jiù shàngbān qùle.
She had some congee and then went to work.

100.3 有的 字 容易 記，有的 很 難 記。
Yǒude zì róngyi jì, yǒude hěn nán jì.
Some characters are easy to remember while others are very hard to remember.

100.4 有的 人 喜歡 吃 辣的，可是 我 一點兒 也 不 喜歡。
Yǒude rén xǐhuan chī làde, kěshi wǒ yìdiǎnr yě bù xǐhuan.
Some people like to eat spicy food, but I don't like to at all.

101. 又 yòu and 再 zài

Both "又 yòu" and "再 zài" can be translated as "again" in English. However there are three points of distinction to note:

(1) We use "又 yòu" to talk about past or completed events and "再 zài" for future events.

101.1 又 碰見 你 了！
Yòu pèngjian nǐ le!
It's you again!

101.2 你 又 叫錯了 我的 名字。
Nǐ yòu jiàocuòle wǒde míngzi.
You've pronounced my name wrong again.

101.3 明天 再 來 談談。
Míngtian zài lái tántan.
Come again to talk about it tomorrow.

101.4 再 坐 一會兒 吧？
Zài zuò yìhuǐr ba?
Won't you stay a little longer?

(2) "又 yòu" may be used to introduce something additional while "再 zài" may not.

101.5 她 是 位 好 老師， 又 是 位 能幹的 母親。
Tā shì wèi hǎo lǎoshī, yòu shì wèi nénggànde mǔqin.
She is a good teacher and also a capable mother.

101.6 天 刮着 大 風， 又 下着 大 雨。
Tiān guāzhe dà fēng, yòu xiàzhe dà yǔ.
It's very windy and also raining heavily.

(3) "再 zài" may be used to indicate a higher degree while "又 yòu" may not.

101.7 你 再 聰明 也 沒用。
Nǐ zài cōngming yě méiyòng.
Even if you were more clever it would still be useless.

101.8 再 大 聲 點兒 可以 嗎？
Zài dà shēng diǎnr kěyǐ ma?
Can you speak even louder?

102. 有點兒 yǒudiǎnr

Typical error:

I'm a bit tired.
我 一點兒 累了。
Wǒ yìdiǎnr lèile.

Correct usage:

我 有 (一)點兒 累了。
Wǒ yǒu (yì)diǎnr lèile.

"有點兒 yǒudiǎnr" is an adverbial, that is, it can be used before an adjective or a verb. We use it to talk about small degrees. It means "somewhat" or "a bit".

102.1 我 有點兒 同意 她的 看法。
Wǒ yǒudiǎnr tóngyì tāde kànfǎ.
I somewhat agree with her viewpoint.

102.2 她 有點兒 傷風。
Tā yǒudiǎnr shāngfēng.
She has a slight cold.

102.3 經理 有點兒 不 滿意 我。
Jīnglǐ yǒudiǎnr bù mǎnyì wǒ.
The manager is somewhat dissatisfied with me.

Note: "有點兒 yǒudiǎnr" may be used as a "verb + measure" construction. As such a construction, it takes a noun after it.

102.4 這 件 事 有點兒 希望。
Zhèi jiàn shì yǒudiǎnr xīwàng.
There's some hope in this matter.

102.5 他 有點兒 經驗。
Tā yǒudiǎnr jīngyàn.
He has some experience.

102.6 我們 能 有點兒 自由 就 好了。
Wǒmen néng yǒudiǎnr zìyóu jiù hǎole.
We'd be better off if we could have some freedom.

Note that when "有點兒 yǒudiǎnr" and "一點兒 yìdiǎnr" are used adverbially, they differ from each other in the following ways:

(1) "一點兒 yìdiǎnr" can be used in imperative sentences (requests, commands, etc.), but "有點兒 yǒudiǎnr" cannot.
(2) "有點兒 yǒudiǎnr" may be used in the structure: "有點兒 + Verb/Adjective" whereas "一點兒 yìdiǎnr" may be used in two structures:

(a) "Adjective + 一點兒 + Verb"

102.7 早 一點兒 來。
Zǎo yìdiǎnr lái.
Come a little earlier.

(b) "Verb + Adjective + 一點兒"

102.8 寫 清楚 一點兒。
Xiě qīngchu yìdiǎnr.
Write a little clearer.

Note: Only such adjectives as "早 zǎo", "晚 wǎn", "快 kuài", and "慢 màn" may appear in both structures. Other adjectives normally employ structure (b).

103. 有意思 yǒuyìsi and 感興趣 gǎn xìngqu

Typical error:

I'm interested in reading.
我 對 看書 有意思。
Wǒ duì kànshū yǒuyìsi.

Correct usage:

我 對 看書 感 興趣。
Wǒ duì kànshū gǎn xìngqu.

"有意思 yǒuyìsi" is an adjective and it means "interesting" or "enjoyable".

103.1 他 這 個 人 真 有意思。
Tā zhèi ge rén zhēn yǒuyìsi.
He is a truly interesting person.

103.2 我們 今天 玩兒得 很 有意思。
Wǒmen jīntian wánrde hěn yǒuyìsi.
We've had a marvelous time today.

Note: The position of "有意思 yǒuyìsi" is normally after a nominal or verbal expression.

"感興趣 gǎn xìngqu" is used when we want to talk about our personal interest. The pattern is "對 + noun (your interest) + 感興趣".

103.3 他 對 釣魚 感 興趣。
Tā duì diàoyú gǎn xìngqu.
He is interested in fishing.

103.4 她 對 跳舞 不 感 興趣。
Tā duì tiàowǔ bù gǎn xìngqu.
She is not interested in dancing.

104. 在 zài (after verbs)

Typical error:

Put it on the table.
放 桌子 上。
Fàng zhuōzi shang.

Correct usage:

放在 桌子 上。
Fàngzài zhuōzi shang.

In Chinese, "在 + location" is mostly used before verbs.
For example:

104.1 他 在 河邊兒 上 釣魚 呢。
Tā zài hébiānr shang diàoyú ne.
He's fishing on the river bank.

104.2 她 在 南京 教 英語。
Tā zài Nánjīng jiāo Yīngyǔ.
She teaches English in Nanjing.

However, in a small number of cases "在 + location" is used directly after verbs.

The kind of verbs which can precede "在 zài" include those which indicate movement, placement and posture. In addition, we can also use verbs which are modified by adverbs of place, such as residence and places of one's birth, growth and death, before "在 + location".

104.3 葉子 掉在 水裏 了。
Yèzi diàozai shuǐli le.
The leaves fell into the water.

104.4 請 把 名字 寫在 這兒。
Qǐng bǎ míngzi xiězài zhèr.
Please write your name here.

104.5 請 你 坐在 這裏。
Qǐng nǐ zuòzai zhèli.
Sit over here, please.

104.6 她 住在 哪兒？
Tā zhùzai nǎr?
Where does she live?

104.7 你 生在 哪兒？
Nǐ shēngzai nǎr?
Where were you born?

105. 早上(晨) zǎoshang(chén) and 上午 shàngwǔ

Typical error:

What time do you get up in the morning?
你 上午 幾 點 鐘 起來？
Nǐ shàngwǔ jǐ diǎn zhōng qǐlai?

Correct usage:

你 早上 幾 點 鐘 起來？
Nǐ zǎoshang jǐ diǎn zhōng qǐlai?

Both "早上 zǎoshang" and "上午 shàngwǔ" can be translated as "morning" in English. However, there is a distinction between them. "早上 zǎoshang" generally refers to early morning from the time around daybreak to eight or nine in the morning, and "上午 shàngwǔ" normally refers to the time between daybreak and twelve noon. In other words, "早上 zǎoshang" is the time when one gets up and drinks one's coffee while reading the paper, while "上午 shàngwǔ" is the whole morning.

Examples:

105.1 她 每天 早上 都 去 跑步。
Tā měitiān zǎoshang dōu qù pǎobù.
She goes jogging every morning.

105.2 她 早上 不 吃 早飯。
Tā zǎoshang bù chī zǎofàn.
She doesn't eat breakfast in the morning.

105.3 你 一 個 上午 都 在 幹 甚麼？
Nǐ yí ge shàngwǔ dōu zài gàn shénme?
What have you been doing all morning?

105.4 你 上午 有 空 嗎？
Nǐ shàngwǔ yǒu kòng ma?
Are you free in the morning?

106. 長 zhǎng and 長得 zhǎngde

Typical error:

He's grown quite tall.
他　長了　真　高。
Tā　zhǎngle　zhēn　gāo.

Correct usage:

他　長得　真　高。
Tā　zhǎngde　zhēn　gāo.

"長 zhǎng" is a verb, which is used to talk about natural growth or physical development.

106.1 他　長　高了　十　公分。
Tā　zhǎng　gāole　shí　gōngfēn.
He has grown ten centimeters in height.

106.2 孩子　長　牙　了。
Háizi　zhǎng　yá　le.
The baby is teething.

106.3 樹　長　葉子　了。
Shù　zhǎng　yèzi　le.
The tree has leaves now.

"長得 zhǎngde" is used to describe the present state of growth of an animate object. Hence, it is generally followed by an "Adverb of degree + Adjective" or an adjective.

106.4 她　長得　真　漂亮。
Tā　zhǎngde　zhēn　piàoliang.
She is truly pretty.

106.5 這　棵　樹　長得　太　高了。
Zhèi　kē　shù　zhǎngde　tài　gāole.
This tree has grown too tall.

106.6 這　孩子　長得　真　像　他　媽媽。
Zhèi　háizi　zhǎngde　zhēn　xiàng　tā　māma.
This child really looks like his mother.

106.7 他　長得　真　結實。
Tā　zhǎngde　zhēn　jiēshi.
He's grown quite strong.

107. 着涼 zhāoliáng, 傷風 shāngfēng, 感冒 gǎnmào, 發燒 fāshāo

When we talk about "a cold" or "a fever", we use verb-object compounds. Generally, we do not use the verb "有 yǒu" before these verb-object compounds. Hence, when we say that somebody has got a cold we would normally say "他着涼了 Tā zhāoliáng le". Note that "着涼 zhāoliáng", "傷風 shāngfēng" and "感冒 gǎnmào" are synonyms.

107.1 一 不 小心， 就 容易 感冒。
Yí bù xiǎoxīn, jiù róngyi gǎnmào.
If you're not careful, it's easy to catch a cold.

107.2 他 昨天 夜裏 發 高燒。
Tā zuótian yèli fā gāoshāo.
Last night he had a high temperature (fever).

107.3 我 傷風得 很 利害。
Wǒ shāngfēngde hěn lìhai.
I've got a bad cold.

108. 着 zhe and 在 zài + verb

"着 zhe" is normally used as a verb suffix, although it can also be preceded by an adjective. Its grammatical function is primarily to signal the continuation of an action or the prolongation of a state (i.e. the result of a completed action). Structurally, "着 zhe" may appear in any one of the following five patterns:

(1) Adverbial + Verb-zhe + (object)

108.1 他 高興 地 走着。
Tā gāoxìng de zǒuzhe.
He is walking happily.

108.2 她 在 屋子裏 看着 報 呢。
Tā zài wūzili kànzhe bào ne.
She is reading the newspaper in the room.

(2) 正 zhèng + Verb-zhe + object + 呢 ne

108.3 外頭 正 下着 雨 呢。
Wàitou zhèng xiàzhe yǔ ne.
It's raining outside.

108.4 我們 正 開着 會 呢。
Wǒmen zhèng kāizhe huì ne.
We are having a meeting now.

(3) $Verb_1$ / Adjective-zhe + $Verb_2$

108.5 他 忙着 跟 人 說話。
Tā mángzhe gēn rén shuōhuà.
He is busy talking with people.

108.6 我 看着 報 吃飯。
Wǒ kànzhe bào chīfàn.
I eat while reading the newspaper.

(4) Inanimate object + Verb-zhe (prolongation of a state)

108.7 門 開着 呢。
Mén kāizhe ne.
The door is open.

108.8 牆上 掛着 一 張 畫兒。
Qiángshang guàzhe yì zhāng huàr.
There is a painting hanging on the wall.

(5) $Verb_1$-zhe $Verb_1$-zhe + $Verb_2$

108.9 她　說着　說着　睡着了。
Tā shuōzhe shuōzhe shuìzháole.
While she was talking, she fell asleep.

108.10 他　想着　想着　笑了起來。
Tā xiǎngzhe xiǎngzhe xiàoleqilai.
While he was thinking, he started to laugh.

Note: The fifth usage of "着 zhe" is usually associated with past events.

When "在 zài" is used before verbs, it indicates a continuous action. It differs from "着 zhe" in that we can use "在 zai", but not "着 zhe ", to answer the question "what is one doing?"

108.11 A: 小　李　在　幹(做)　甚麼？
Xiǎo Lǐ zài gàn(zuò) shénme?
What is little Li doing?

B: 他　在　吃飯。(*not* 他吃着飯。)
Tā zài chīfàn.
He's eating.

108.12 你　在　寫　甚麼？ (*not* 你寫着甚麼？)
Nǐ zài xiě shénme?
What are you writing?

108.13 她　在　唸書　呢。
Tā zài niànshū ne.
She's studying.

Note: "在 zài" may take the particle "呢 ne" at the end of a sentence.

109. 這 zhèi and 那 nèi

When students of Chinese use these two specifiers, they often confuse the Chinese listener by using "那 nèi" (that) for people or things which are physically close to the speaker. There are at least two reasons for confusing "那 nèi" with "這 zhèi". First, the English demonstrative "that" is used more often than "this". Second, in a number of situations, the English speaker would use "that" while the Chinese speaker would use "this" or he would simply depend on the context to indicate someone or something which is close to him in space, time or thought.

109.1 這 才 是 好 孩子！
Zhèi cái shì hǎo háizi!
That's a dear!

109.2 別 這樣 看 我。
Bié zhèiyàng kàn wǒ.
Don't look at me like that.

109.3 這 本 書 多少 錢？
Zhèi běn shū duōshǎo qián?
How much does that book cost? (The listener holds the book and is within talking distance with the speaker.)

109.4 (這個) 味兒 真 香。
(Zhèige) wèir zhēn xiāng.
That smells nice.

109.5 這個 故事 真 好聽。
Zhèige gùshi zhēn hǎotīng.
That's a good story.

110. 値錢 zhíqián and 値得 zhíde

We use "值錢 zhíqián" to talk about things which are valuable or expensive. We do not use it for abstract concepts such as time, human life, etc. To describe such abstract concepts we use "寶貴 bǎoguì" (valuable).

110.1 他的 古玩 很 值錢。
Tāde gǔwán hěn zhíqián.
His antique is very valuable.

110.2 她 有 一 件 值錢的 首飾。
Tā yǒu yí jiàn zhíqiánde shǒushi.
She has an expensive piece of jewelery.

We use "值得 zhíde" to describe something which is worthwhile or worth doing.

110.3 這 本 書 值得 看。
Zhèi běn shū zhíde kàn.
This book is worth reading.

110.4 這 是 一 件 值得 注意的 事。
Zhèi shì yí jiàn zhíde zhùyìde shì.
That's something noteworthy.

111. 重 zhòng and 厚 hòu

We use "重 zhòng" to describe something which is heavy in weight. It can also be used in an abstract sense. "厚 hòu" is used to describe something which is thick.

Examples of "重 zhòng" and "厚 hòu":

111.1 他的 上海 口音 很 重。
Tāde Shànghǎi kǒuyīn hěn zhòng.
He has a marked/heavy Shanghainese accent.

111.2 我們的 工作 不 重。
Wǒmende gōngzuò bú zhòng.
Our work load is not heavy.

111.3 雪 挺 厚 的。
Xuě tǐng hòu de.
The snow is rather deep.

111.4 他 是 個 厚臉皮。
Tā shì ge hòuliǎnpí.
He is a brazen person.

Note that "重 zhòng" cannot be used in the English sense of "heavy" as in "heavy breakfast" and "heavy clothing". The Chinese equivalents to these two expressions are:

111.5 我 吃了 一 頓 豐富(rich)的 早飯。
Wǒ chīle yí dùn fēngfùde zǎofàn.
I had a heavy breakfast.

111.6 天氣 涼了， 你 最好 穿 件 厚 點兒 的 衣服。
Tiānqi liángle, nǐ zuìhǎo chuān jiàn hòu diǎnr de yīfu.
The weather has turned cooler. You'd better wear something heavier.

112. 字 zì and 句 jù

When English speakers use such expressions as "in a word", "a few words" and "in other words" the Chinese equivalent is not "字 zì" (character), but "句(話) jù(huà)" (sentence).

112.1 我 會 說 幾 句 漢語。
Wǒ huì shuō jǐ jù Hànyǔ.
I can speak a few words of Chinese.

112.2 一 句 話，我 不 願意 去。
Yí jù huà, wǒ bú yuànyi qù.
In a word, I don't want to go.

112.3 換 句 話 說，她 今天 不 來了。
Huàn jù huà shuō, tā jīntian bù láile.
In other words, she's not coming today.

112.4 他 就 會 說 幾 個 英文 單 字。
Tā jiù huì shuō jǐ ge Yīngwén dān zì.
He can only speak a few simple English words.

113. 走 zǒu, 走走 zǒuzǒu, 走路 zǒulù, 走着 zǒuzhe

Typical error:

He walks to your place.
他 走 去 你 家。
Tā zǒu qù nǐ jiā.

Correct usage:

他 走路/走着 去 你 家。
Tā zǒulù/zǒuzhe qù nǐ jiā.

"走 zǒu" is primarily used in the sense of "to walk", "to go" or "to leave".

113.1 他 走得 快，我 走得 慢。
Tā zǒude kuài, wǒ zǒude màn.
He walks quickly and I walk slowly.

113.2 到 他 家 去，怎麼 走？
Dào tā jiā qù, zěnme zǒu?
How do you get to his place?

113.3 坐 船 去 得 走 幾 天？
Zuò chuán qù děi zǒu jǐ tiān?
How long does it take to go by boat?

113.4 我們 幾 點 鐘 走？
Wǒmen jǐ diǎn zhōng zǒu?
What time do we leave?

113.5 我們 不 該 "走 後門"。
Wǒmen bù gāi "zǒu hòumén".
We should not "enter by the back door" (i.e. secure advantages through connections).

"走走 zǒuzǒu" is an idiom, which means "to take a walk".

113.6 吃完飯 我們 去 走走。
Chīwánfàn wǒmen qù zǒuzǒu.
Let's take a walk after we eat.

"走路 zǒulù" is a verb-object compound. We normally use it adverbially, in the sense of "on foot". It can also be used as a nominal expression, in the sense of "walking".

113.7 我們 走路 去 還是 坐車 去？
Wǒmen zǒulù qù háishì zuòchē qù?
Are we walking or taking the bus?

113.8 走路 旅行 很 累。
Zǒulù lǚxíng hěn lèi.
Travelling by foot is very tiring.

113.9 走路 對 身體 好。
Zǒulù duì shēntǐ hǎo.
Walking is good for your health.

"走着 zǒuzhe" can also be used adverbially to indicate getting to a place "by foot".

113.10 我們 走着 去 吧。
Wǒmen zǒuzhe qù ba.
Let's walk there.

114. 走 zǒu, 去 qù, 離開 líkāi

Typical error:

When are you going to Japan?
你們　甚麼　時候　走　日本？
Nǐmen　shénme　shíhou　zǒu　Rìběn?

Correct usage:

你們　甚麼　時候　去　日本？
Nǐmen　shénme　shíhou　qù　Rìběn?

We may either use "走 zǒu" or "去 qù" to mean "go" or "leave". However, "走 zǒu" cannot take a place word after it whereas "去 qù" can.

114.1　他們　是　哪　年　走／去　的？
Tāmen　shì　něi　nián　zǒu/qù　de?
In what year did they leave?

114.2　我們　明天　要　去　德國。
Wǒmen　míngtian　yào　qù　Déguó.
We're going to Germany tomorrow.

"走 zǒu" is unacceptable here. Although "走 zǒu", "去 qù" and "離開 líkāi" bear the same meaning "leave", only "離開 líkāi" can take a place word after it.

114.3　你　甚麼　時候　離開　香港？
Nǐ　shénme　shíhou　líkāi　Xiānggǎng?
When are you leaving Hong Kong?

Both "走 zǒu" and "去 qù" are unacceptable here.

114.4　他們　一　家　不　久　就　會　離開　這兒　到　英國　去。
Tāmen　yì　jiā　bù　jiǔ　jiù　huì　líkāi　zhèr　dào　Yīngguó　qù.
Their whole family will soon leave here for England.

114.5　我們　一定　得　早　點兒　走／去／離開。
Wǒmen　yídìng　děi　zǎo　diǎnr　zǒu/qù/líkāi.
We must leave early.

APPENDIX
Pinyin-Yale-Wade Comparative Table

Pinyin	Yale	Wade-Giles	Pinyin	Yale	Wade-Giles
a	a	a	ceng	tseng	ts'eng
ai	ai	ai	cha	cha	ch'a
an	an	an	chai	chai	ch'ai
ang	ang	ang	chan	chan	ch'an
ao	au	ao	chang	chang	ch'ang
			chao	chau	ch'ao
ba	ba	pa	che	che	ch'e
bai	bai	pai	chen	chen	ch'en
ban	ban	pan	cheng	cheng	ch'eng
bang	bang	pang	chi	chr	ch'ih
bao	bau	pao	chong	chung	ch'ung
bei	bei	pei	chou	chou	ch'ou
ben	ben	pen	chu	chu	ch'u
beng	beng	peng	chuai	chwai	ch'uai
bi	bi	pi	chuan	chwan	ch'uan
bian	byan	pien	chuang	chwang	ch'uang
biao	byau	piao	chui	chwei	ch'ui
bie	bye	pieh	chun	chwun	ch'un
bin	bin	pin	chuo	chwo	ch'o
bing	bing	ping	ci	tsz	tz'u
bo	bwo	po	cong	tsung	ts'ung
bou	bou	pou	cou	tsou	ts'ou
bu	bu	pu	cu	tsu	ts'u
			cuan	tswan	ts'uan
ca	tsa	ts'a	cui	tswei	ts'ui
cai	tsai	ts'ai	cun	tswun	ts'un
can	tsan	ts'an	cuo	tswo	ts'o
cang	tsang	ts'ang			
cao	tsau	ts'ao	da	da	ta
ce	tse	ts'e	dai	dai	tai
cen	tsen	ts'en	dan	dan	tan

Pinyin	Yale	Wade-Giles
dang	dang	tang
dao	dau	tao
de	de	te
dei	dei	tei
deng	deng	teng
di	di	ti
dian	dyan	tien
diao	dyau	tiao
die	dye	tieh
ding	ding	ting
diu	dyou	tiu
dong	dung	tung
dou	dou	tou
du	du	tu
duan	dwan	tuan
dui	dwei	tui
dun	dwun	tun
duo	dwo	to
e	e	e, o
ei	ei	ei
en	en	en
eng	eng	eng
er	er	erh
fa	fa	fa
fan	fan	fan
fang	fang	fang
fei	fei	fei
fen	fen	fen
feng	feng	feng
fo	fwo	fo
fou	fou	fou
fu	fu	fu
ga	ga	ka
gai	gai	kai

Pinyin	Yale	Wade-Giles
gan	gan	kan
gang	gang	kang
gao	gau	kao
ge	ge	ke, ko
gei	gei	kei
gen	gen	ken
geng	geng	keng
gong	gung	kung
gou	gou	kou
gu	gu	ku
gua	gwa	kua
guai	gwai	kuai
guan	gwan	kuan
guang	gwang	kuang
gui	gwei	kuei
gun	gwun	kun
guo	gwo	kuo
ha	ha	ha
hai	hai	hai
han	han	han
hang	hang	hang
hao	hau	hao
he	he	ho
hei	hei	hei
hen	hen	hen
heng	heng	heng
hong	hung	hung
hou	hou	hou
hu	hu	hu
hua	hwa	hua
huai	hwai	huai
huan	hwan	huan
huang	hwang	huang
hui	hwei	hui
hun	hwun	hun
huo	hwo	huo

Pinyin	Yale	Wade-Giles
ji	ji	chi
jia	jya	chia
jian	jyan	chien
jiang	jyang	chiang
jiao	jyau	chiao
jie	jye	chieh
jin	jin	chin
jing	jing	ching
jiong	jyung	chiung
jiu	jyou	chiu
ju	jyu	chü
juan	jywan	chüan
jue	jywe	chüeh
jun	jyun	chün
ka	ka	k'a
kai	kai	k'ai
kan	kan	k'an
kang	kang	k'ang
kao	kau	k'ao
ke	ke	k'e, k'o
ken	ken	k'en
keng	keng	k'eng
kong	kung	k'ung
kou	kou	k'ou
ku	ku	k'u
kua	kwa	k'ua
kuai	kwai	k'uai
kuan	kwan	k'uan
kuang	kwang	k'uang
kui	kwei	k'uei
kun	kwun	k'un
kuo	kwo	k'uo
la	la	la
lai	lai	lai
lan	lan	lan

Pinyin	Yale	Wade-Giles
lang	lang	lang
lao	lau	lao
le	le	le
lei	lei	lei
leng	leng	leng
li	li	li
lia	lya	lia
lian	lyan	lien
liang	lyang	liang
liao	lyau	liao
lie	lye	lieh
lin	lin	lin
ling	ling	ling
liu	lyou	liu
long	lung	lung
lou	lou	lou
lu	lu	lu
lü	lyu	lü
luan	lwan	luan
lüan	lywan	lüan
lüe	lywe	lüeh
lun	lwun	lun
luo	lwo	lo
ma	ma	ma
mai	mai	mai
man	man	man
mang	mang	mang
mao	mau	mao
mei	mei	mei
men	men	men
meng	meng	meng
mi	mi	mi
mian	myan	mien
miao	myau	miao
mie	mye	mieh
min	min	min

Pinyin	Yale	Wade-Giles
ming	ming	ming
miu	myou	miu
mo	mwo	mo
mou	mou	mou
mu	mu	mu
na	na	na
nai	nai	nai
nan	nan	nan
nang	nang	nang
nao	nau	nao
ne	ne	ne
nei	nei	nei
nen	nen	nen
neng	neng	neng
ni	ni	ni
nian	nyan	nien
niang	nyang	niang
niao	nyau	niao
nie	nye	nieh
nin	nin	nin
ning	ning	ning
niu	nyou	niu
nong	nung	nung
nou	nou	nou
nu	nu	nu
nü	nyu	nü
nuan	nwan	nuan
nüe	nywe	nüeh
nun	nwun	nun
nuo	nwo	no
ou	ou	ou
pa	pa	p’a
pai	pai	p’ai
pan	pan	p’an

Pinyin	Yale	Wade-Giles
pang	pang	p’ang
pao	pau	p’ao
pei	pei	p’ei
pen	pen	p’en
peng	peng	p’eng
pi	pi	p’i
pian	pyan	p’ien
piao	pyau	p’iao
pie	pye	p’ieh
pin	pin	p’in
ping	ping	p’ing
po	pwo	p’o
pou	pou	p’ou
pu	pu	p’u
qi	chi	ch’i
qia	chya	ch’ia
qian	chyan	ch’ien
qiang	chyang	ch’iang
qiao	chyau	ch’iao
qie	chye	ch’ieh
qin	chin	ch’in
qing	ching	ch’ing
qiong	chyung	ch’iung
qiu	chyou	ch’iu
qu	chyu	ch’ü
quan	chywan	ch’üan
que	chywe	ch’üeh
qun	chyun	ch’ün
ran	ran	jan
rang	rang	jang
rao	rau	jao
re	re	je
ren	ren	jen
reng	reng	jeng
ri	r	jih

Pinyin	Yale	Wade-Giles
rong	rung	jung
rou	rou	jou
ru	ru	ju
ruan	rwan	juan
rui	rwei	jui
run	rwun	jun
ruo	rwo	jo
sa	sa	sa
sai	sai	sai
san	san	san
sang	sang	sang
sao	sau	sao
se	se	se
sen	sen	sen
seng	seng	seng
sha	sha	sha
shai	shai	shai
shan	shan	shan
shang	shang	shang
shao	shau	shao
she	she	she
shei	shei	shei
shen	shen	shen
sheng	sheng	sheng
shi	shr	shih
shou	shou	shou
shu	shu	shu
shua	shwa	shua
shuai	shwai	shuai
shuan	shwan	shuan
shuang	shwang	shuang
shui	shwei	shui
shun	shwun	shun
shuo	shwo	shuo
si	sz	ssu, szu
song	sung	sung

Pinyin	Yale	Wade-Giles
sou	sou	sou
su	su	su
suan	swan	suan
sui	swei	sui
sun	swun	sun
suo	swo	so
ta	ta	t'a
tai	tai	t'ai
tan	tan	t'an
tang	tang	t'ang
tao	tau	t'ao
te	te	t'e
teng	teng	t'eng
ti	ti	t'i
tian	tyan	t'ien
tiao	tyau	t'iao
tie	tye	t'ieh
ting	ting	t'ing
tong	tung	t'ung
tou	tou	t'ou
tu	tu	t'u
tuan	twan	t'uan
tui	twei	t'ui
tun	twun	t'un
tuo	two	t'o
wa	wa	wa
wai	wai	wai
wan	wan	wan
wang	wang	wang
wei	wei	wei
wen	wen	wen
weng	weng	weng
wo	wo	wo
wu	wu	wu

Pinyin	Yale	Wade-Giles
xi	syi	hsi
xia	sya	hsia
xian	syan	hsien
xiang	syang	hsiang
xiao	syau	hsiao
xie	sye	hsieh
xin	syin	hsin
xing	sying	hsing
xiong	syung	hsiung
xiu	syou	hsiu
xu	syu	hsü
xuan	sywan	hsüan
xue	sywe	hsüeh
xun	syun	hsün
ya	ya	ya
yai	yai	yai
yan	yan	yen
yang	yang	yang
yao	yau	yao
ye	ye	yeh
yi	yi	yi, i
yin	yin	yin
ying	ying	ying
yong	yung	yung
you	you	yu
yu	yu	yü
yuan	ywan	yüan
yue	ywe	yüeh
yun	yun	yün
za	dza	tsa
zai	dzai	tsai
zan	dzan	tsan

Pinyin	Yale	Wade-Giles
zang	dzang	tsang
zao	dzau	tsao
ze	dze	tse
zei	dzei	tsei
zen	dzen	tsen
zeng	dzeng	tseng
zha	ja	cha
zhai	jai	chai
zhan	jan	chan
zhang	jang	chang
zhao	jau	chao
zhe	je	che
zhei	jei	chei
zhen	jen	chen
zheng	jeng	cheng
zhi	jr	chih
zhong	jung	chung
zhou	jou	chou
zhu	ju	chu
zhua	jwa	chua
zhuai	jwai	chuai
zhuan	jwan	chuan
zhuang	jwang	chuang
zhui	jwei	chui
zhun	jwun	chun
zhuo	jwo	cho
zi	dz	tzu
zong	dzung	tsung
zou	dzou	tsou
zu	dzu	tsu
zuan	dzwan	tsuan
zui	dzwei	tsui
zun	dzwun	tsun
zuo	dzwo	tso

Exercises

Exercise 1

Use 吧，嗎 or 呢 in these sentences:

1. 讓我們談談___。
2. 你怎麼來晚了___？
3. 她不會不去___？
4. 你先生最近忙___？
5. 他結婚了，你___？
6. 這句話的意思不是很清楚___？
7. 小李到底願意不願意去旅行___？
8. 她大概已經上班了___？

Exercise 2

Change these sentences into the 把 construction:

1. 她吃了我昨天買的糖。
2. 我找錢給他了。
3. 孩子洗手洗得乾淨極了。
4. 你一定要學好中文。
5. 回家後練練歌兒。
6. 這件事，你千萬別告訴她。

Exercise 3

Use 半，一半 or 一個半 in these sentences:

1. 他才___歲。
2. 她開會開了___就走了。
3. 還剩下___個蘋果，另外___我吃了。
4. 書的___是她寫的，___是我寫的。
5. $1\frac{1}{2}$ 月是___月。

Exercise 4

Use 幫 or 幫忙 in these sentences:

1. 我來___你。
2. 請___我找一下我的狗。
3. 請你___開開門。
4. 她___做菜。
5. 他___組織了一個足球隊。

Exercise 5

Translate the " 倍 " in these sentences into English:

1. 她的錢比我的多兩倍。
2. 我的歲數有他的兩倍。
3. 他的房子是我的三倍大。
4. 她住的地方比我那兒遠一倍半。

Exercise 6 (比)

Rearrange the order of the following words so as to make them meaningful sentences:

1. 我妹妹高比多了
2. 他爸爸小比 20 歲
3. 日本車貴比德國車得多
4. 弟弟我矮比一點兒

Exercise 7 (畢業)

Translate the following into Chinese:

1. When are you graduating from high school?
2. After graduating from college, he went to graduate school.

Exercise 8 (別客氣)

Translate the following into Chinese:

1. Please make yourself at home.
2. Thank you for your help. You're welcome.
3. Please don't bother. I'm not thirsty.

Exercise 9

Supply 別的 or 另外 in the following:

1. __一本書是他買的。
2. 我__還要到桂林去。
3. 咱們說__吧。
4. 他不買__，就買貴的。
5. 她__一隻眼睛看不清楚。

Exercise 10

Supply 不 or 別 in the following:

1. 他__想出去玩兒。
2. __出去！
3. 我__太累。
4. __不好意思嘛。
5. 我__一定喜歡她。

Exercise 11 (想……不，不想，不覺得，不認爲)

Translate the following into Chinese:

1. I don't think she is coming.
2. We don't feel that is right.
3. I don't feel like going out today.
4. Don't you think it's going to rain?
5. She doesn't miss home.

Exercise 12 (才)

Translate the following into Chinese:

1. You are a thief, you are?
2. He just sat down.
3. I've studied Chinese for only one month.

Exercise 13

Use 長 or 久 in these sentences:

1. 這條褲子不夠__。
2. 我們等得夠__了。
3. 他玩的時間太__了。
4. 你來了有多__？

Exercise 14

Supply 吃不(得)下，吃不(得)了 or 吃不(得)着(到) in the following:

1. 今天太累了，__飯。
2. 菜這麼多，我一個人怎麼__？
3. 在美國__四川菜嗎？
4. 在他家__水果嗎？
5. 大魚__小魚嗎？

Exercise 15

Use 出事 or 意外 in these sentences:

1. 你開車__嗎？
2. 爲甚麼飛機常發生__？
3. __了甚麼__？
4. 那孩子騎車又__了。
5. 他講給我們聽__是怎麼發生的。

Exercise 16

Use 從來没(不) or 一直没(不) in these sentences:

1. 我__戴眼鏡。
2. 我__見過她。
3. 今年我__見過她。
4. 我__吃肉，到了中國以後，也__吃過。

Exercise 17

Use 大家 or 每個人 in these sentences:

1. __請注意，火車就快開了。
2. 別客氣，__一塊兒吃吧。
3. 他們__都有一本字典。
4. 他們__都回家了。
5. __的事，__做。
6. 老師到__的家裏去了解情況

Exercise 18

Use 拿 or 帶 in these sentences:

1. 他__我的錢去買書去了。
2. 你__甚麼東西來了？

3. 請把那份報__給我看看。
4. 你__女朋友去參加晚會嗎？
5. 到北方去一定得多__些衣服。
6. 你__護照 (passport) 了嗎？

Exercise 19

Use appropriate adjectives in the following:

1. 她美倒是__，可是很聰明。
2. 這孩子__是挺聰明，就是太愛玩兒。
3. 老師厲害倒是__，但是很關心我們。
4. 這個東西貴倒__，可是樣子不好看。
5. 他做事慢倒有點兒__，可是很仔細。

Exercise 20 (Verb + 到)

Translate the following into Chinese:

1. He received a parcel yesterday.
2. How far have you read it?
3. Have you heard that news?
4. I thought of you yesterday.
5. Did you smell it?
6. Have you discussed up to the third point yet?

Exercise 21

Use "+" to indicate " 的 " is required and "–" to indicate " 的 " is not required:

1. 好__人，壞__人都有。
2. 藍藍__天，綠綠__海，真美麗。
3. 他是個最麻煩__人。
4. 大__人，小__孩子都可以參加。
5. 衣服的顏色有很多種，有紅__，黃__，藍__等等。
6. 她長着一雙大大__眼睛。

Exercise 22

Supply (定) 約會，掛號 or 約 in these sentences:

1. 你跟他們__了幾點？
2. 這是我第一次跟女朋友__。
3. 你的信要不要__？
4. 你要__誰去看電影？
5. 内科__的時間是早上九點。
6. 我下午有一個__，所以去不了。

Exercise 23

Supply 東西 or 事情 in these sentences:

1. 你這個壞__！
2. 這是大家的__，應該大家辦。
3. 這件__誰負責？
4. 你就懂得吃好__。
5. 快點兒收拾一下__。

Exercise 24 (都)

Translate the following into Chinese:

1. All the boys want you to tell a story.
2. Are you all here?
3. Tell us all you know about it.
4. I have looked all over for him.
5. It's all done.
6. Her face is all red.

Exercise 25

Supply 對不起，請問 or 勞駕 in the following:

1. __，讓我們過去。
2. __，我叫錯了你的名字。
3. __，中國有幾條大河？
4. __，把菜單給我看看。
5. 他撞了人怎麼不說"__"？

Exercise 26

Supply 對 or 跟 in these sentences:

1. 你去__他談談吧。
2. 我__他們先研究一下再說。
3. 他__誰都沒禮貌。
4. 學生__老師的態度好。
5. 小李__你有很多意見。

Exercise 27 (多)

Translate the following into Chinese:

1. He bought one hat too many.
2. Kindly give us your advice.
3. We hope to see more of this city.
4. I've been teaching for more than twenty years.
5. The more, the better.

Exercise 28

Supply 二 or 兩 in the following:

1. __個人得給__十塊錢。
2. $2\frac{1}{2}$ 鐘頭是__個半鐘頭。
3. 3,200 是三千__百。
4. __天就可以到上海了。

Exercise 29

Supply 飯、米 or 菜 in these sentences:

1. 四個__，一個湯，够了。
2. 用上海__做__好吃。
3. 這個__叫甚麼名字？
4. 再給我們來兩碗__ __。
5. 多吃__，少吃__。

Exercise 30

Use 放假 or 假期 in these sentences:

1. 一月一號是__嗎？
2. 你__的時候做些甚麼？
3. __太久了也沒意思。
4. 你們一年有幾天__？
5. 春__你們__幾天？

Exercise 31

Use 方便 or 順便 in these sentences:

1. 你洗碗的時候，__洗一下我的杯子。
2. 請你__把門關上。
3. 不忙，你__的時候給我找一下那本書。
4. 時間對你們__嗎？
5. 他就想到自己的__。

Exercise 32

Supply 剛才 or 剛 (剛) in the following:

1. 他__開始學漢語，還說不好。
2. __下雨的時候，你在哪兒？
3. 我__到這兒，還沒機會去玩玩呢。
4. 她__對我說，她不去日本了。
5. 我離開美國__一個月。

Exercise 33 (Verb + 給)

Translate the following into Chinese:

1. He bought her a watch.
2. Can you lend me three hundred dollars?
3. She is going to give me some new stamps.
4. I sold my car to him. (Use 把 construction)
5. To whom did you hand the letter? (Use 把 construction)

Exercise 34

Supply 跟 or 也 in the following:

1. 我喜歡跳舞__唱歌。
2. 他愛吃魚，__愛吃羊肉。
3. 小李__我都不會游泳。
4. 你__反對他的主意嗎？
5. 我__在寫信呢。
6. 你長高了，__長得更美了。

Exercise 35 (夠)

Translate the following into Chinese:

1. Do we have enough time or not?
2. The rice is still undercooked.
3. That's enough!
4. The food is not enough for six people.
5. The situation there is serious enough.

Exercise 36

Use 關於 or 對於 in these sentences:

1. __這種人，我們應該同情。
2. 他寫的小說是__一個留學生。
3. __中國的風俗習慣，她向來很感興趣。
4. __修理飛機，他知道的很少。
5. 我愛看__歷史的電影。

Exercise 37 (過)

Translate the following into Chinese:

1. Have you driven a car before?
2. Have you ever falling in love with someone?
3. We'll go home after we finished shopping.

Exercise 38

Use 還是 or 或者/或是 in these sentences:

1. 你大__她大？
2. 貴的__便宜的，都行。
3. 你自己決定去__不去。
4. 她是你太太__女朋友？
5. __你決定好。

Exercise 39 (會)

Translate the following into Chinese:

1. She is very good at cooking.
2. Will they get married?
3. Can you speak Cantonese?
4. I can't drive.

Exercise 40 (Inclusives and Exclusives with 甚麼，哪兒，誰)

Translate the following into Chinese:

1. He didn't go anywhere.
2. I don't want to see anyone today.
3. She didn't say anything.
4. I love all kinds of fish.
5. She said that she would like to see all the places.
6. Everybody has their own problems.
7. I'm not going anywhere tonight.

Exercise 41

Use 家 or 房子 in these sentences:

1. 你們__裏有幾個人？
2. __都有自己的問題。
3. 這是我們新買的__。
4. 你們的__比我們的大。

Exercise 42 (借，借給，跟……借)

Translate the following into Chinese:

1. She borrowed a radio yesterday.
2. Don't lend him anything.
3. They didn't borrow anything from us.
4. May I borrow your bag?

Exercise 43

Use 接 or 接到 in these sentences:

1. 你去__她的飛機了沒有？
2. 沒人來__你們嗎？
3. 我沒__你的信。
4. 快去__一下電話。
5. 你__你朋友沒有？

Exercise 44

Use 記得 or 記住 in these sentences:

1. 我__他小時候最愛種花兒。
2. 我__不__這麼久的事了。
3. 請__這個字的發音。
4. 你還__我的生日嗎？
5. 你__這麼多事情嗎？

Exercise 45 (就)

Translate the following into Chinese:

1. I only have one friend.
2. They'll be here in a minute.
3. We'll get off from work at 4:00 p.m. (earlier than usual)
4. I'll come over right after dinner.

Exercise 46

Supply 才 or 就 in the following:

1. 現在__十二點，還太早。
2. 我們都不會說英語，__他會說。
3. 他們__搬了兩張桌子，我一個人__搬了三張。
4. 張先生十年前__畢業了。
5. 張先生是四年前__離開台灣的。
6. 我講了好幾遍，他__明白。

Exercise 47

Use 看，見 or 看見 in these sentences:

1. __，他來了。
2. 我到這兒來是來__朋友的。
3. 他抬頭一__，__了一架飛機。
4. 張校長，有人想__您。
5. 你__我孩子了嗎？
6. 請你來__我母親。
7. 你自己去__就知道了。
8. 你__甚麼報？

Exercise 48

Use 課 or 班 in these sentences:

1. 這個__人太多。
2. 你們一天上幾節__？
3. 請打開第一__。
4. 誰是__長？
5. 你是哪個__的學生？

Exercise 49

Supply 可憐 or 可惜 in the following:

1. 後來他媽媽也死了。他真__。
2. 你不值得__。
3. 真__，我沒能參加你們的婚禮。
4. 丟了這麼點錢，不算__。
5. __他沒念完大學。

Exercise 50 (可以)

Translate the following into Chinese:

1. You may sit down.
2. You can take my car.
3. Can you get to Shanghai by boat?
4. Smoking is not allowed here.

Exercise 51

Use 恐怕 or 怕 in these sentences:

1. 我最__黑。
2. __要下雨了。
3. 她不__吃苦。
4. __你弄錯了吧。
5. 你__我嗎？

Exercise 52 (了)

Translate the following into Chinese:

1. They are not coming now.
2. She is getting prettier and prettier.
3. I've been doing it for years.
4. Terrific!
5. I went to that restaurant yesterday.

Exercise 53

Use 過 or 了 in these sentences:

1. 你去__黄山嗎？
2. 她從來没喝__“龍井茶”。
3. 東西又貴__。
4. 他回__家就看電視。
5. 我學習漢語已經學__一年__。
6. 要是她去__，就一定會碰見我們。
7. 你吃__飯__嗎？
8. 你没出__國吧？
9. 你打__太太嗎？
10. 快把湯喝__。

Exercise 54

Supply 離 or 從 in the following:

1. __明天起，我去學日文。
2. __這裏三里，有一個郵政局。
3. 他的看法__青年人的太遠了。
4. 請你__第一頁念到第三頁。
5. __他遠遠的！
6. __南到北，__東到西，人人都知道我們的東西好。

Exercise 55

Supply 離得(不)開 or 走得(不)開 in the following:

1. 魚__水。
2. 你__女朋友嗎？
3. 五點半以後，我就__了。
4. 現在不太忙，我__。
5. 孩子長大了就__家了。

Exercise 56 (連……都[也])

Translate the following into Chinese:

1. He doesn't even know how to cook.
2. She can even speak French.
3. I forget even his last name.
4. He wouldn't even listen to his wife.
5. Oh, poor thing! You don't even have a dime?

Exercise 57

Supply 忙甚麼，不忙 or 別忙 in these sentences:

1. __？吃完飯再走。
2. __，我們有的是時間。
3. __，他馬上就到了。
4. __，等你有時間我們再去聽音樂。
5. 你在__呢？
6. __，以後有機會再說吧。

Exercise 58 (没關係)

Translate the following into Chinese:

1. It doesn't matter whether she comes or not.
2. Who says stealing isn't a big deal?
3. Never mind! I can do it by myself.
4. It doesn't matter whether it's big or small.
5. It doesn't matter that she didn't phone.

Exercise 59
(Modifier + de + [Specifier] Noun)

Translate the following into Chinese:

1. The book that he is reading was written by my teacher.
2. The food we had in that restaurant yesterday was Sichuan food.
3. The newspaper that he bought is an English daily.
4. This is the place where I was born.
5. What's your favourite sport?

Exercise 60

Use 拿起來，撿起來 or 拿上來 in the following:

1. 把手套（在地上）__。
2. 他從桌子上__書來就走。
3. 把衣服從樓下__。
4. 請把書（在桌上）__念。
5. 他把那塊石頭__扔在河裏了。

Exercise 61

Use 呢 or 嗎 in these sentences:

1. 你爲甚麼不說__？
2. 她可不笨__。
3. 她不笨__。
4. 他在做甚麼__？
5. 他在唸書__？

Exercise 62（能）

Translate the following into Chinese:

1. Can you get here by train?
2. Can you come early?
3. Can I go out and play?
4. I can't talk today.

Exercise 63

Use 會，可以 or 能 in these sentences:

1. 他不__弄錯的，放心吧！
2. 你們__先去，等一會兒我就來。
3. 你__跑多快？
4. 在圖書館裏不__大聲兒說話。
5. 這東西__吃嗎？
6. 我__借你們的電話用嗎？
7. 你__做西餐嗎？
8. 她一定__回來的。
9. 你__打敗他嗎？
10. 他們今天__不__打球？

Exercise 64

Use 年，月，星期 or 日 in these sentences:

1. Wednesday July 1, 1991.
2. What's the date today?
3. What day is today?
4. What month is last month?

Exercise 65

Use 唸，看 or 讀 in these sentences:

1. __書的時候，不要大聲__。
2. 你今年__幾年級？
3. 你可以__她的信，可是不可以__。
4. __書比做事有意思嗎？

Exercise 66

Use 派，送 or 寄 in the following:

1. (是)政府__你到中國去工作的嗎？
2. 這封信，你自己去__，還是__人去__？
3. 他要__孩子進一所有名的學校去學習。
4. 請你把這個禮物__到她家，好嗎？
5. 公司__人到他家去修理水管子。
6. 你__掛號信還是平信？

Exercise 67

Use 碰，碰見，碰到 or 碰上 in these sentences:

1. 別__那部電腦。
2. 小心__頭。
3. 學習外語難免會__很多困難。
4. 我又__了我不願意看見的人。
5. 她在旅行的時候，不幸__了一個賊。
6. 他要到賭場去__運氣。
7. 他們的船__了大風。
8. 在電影院裏，她__了我弟弟。

Exercise 68

Use 碰見/遇見 or 見面 in these sentences:

1. 我們__嗎？
2. 昨天我__了一個老朋友。
3. 他們約好在學校__。
4. 小心__壞人。

Exercise 69

Use 輕 or 薄 in these sentences:

1. 這東西拿着很__。
2. 我喜歡聽__音樂。
3. 衣服太__，不夠暖和。
4. 航空信紙很__，所以__。
5. 你臉皮才不__呢！

Exercise 70

Use 請 or 請客 in the following:

1. 昨天她__我吃北京菜。
2. 你__，爲甚麼没__我？
3. 中國朋友__我們去北海公園去玩兒。
4. 今天我__，我來付錢。
5. 他們__我去演講。
6. 誰__吃喜糖？

Exercise 71

Supply 請 or 請問 in the following:

1. __，美國一共有多少州？
2. __自己來，別客氣。
3. __注意，飛機馬上就要降落了。
4. __，您多大歲數了？
5. 有問題，__隨便問。
6. __跟着我說。
7. 您__坐。
8. __，現在幾點了？

Exercise 72

Supply 請，問 or 叫 in the following:

1. __你太太跟孩子有時間來玩兒。
2. 他__我告訴你他要開會不能來。
3. 我小聲兒地__她幾點鐘。
4. 有問題，__他自己來__我。
5. 經理__你現在去見見他。
6. 他__我去不去游泳。

Exercise 73

Supply the right question words in the following:

1. __對這個工作感興趣，__就可以來試試。
2. __有魚，我就到__去釣。
3. __有錢__請客。
4. __便宜我買__。
5. __個大我要__個。
6. 你們是__決定的，我們就__做。
7. 他__時候有空兒，我們就__時候去找他。
8. 這句話是__說的__知道。
9. 美麗的公主在__，王子就在__。
10. __學快，我就__學。

Exercise 74

(Reduplication of Verbs and Adjectives)

Translate the following into Chinese:

1. We want to have a rest.
2. Would you tidy up the room, please?
3. He returned home happily.
4. Please try it.
5. Let me have a look at your pictures.
6. Wash your hands first.
7. It was blowing gently.
8. Say it slowly, please.

Exercise 75

Use 人 or 男人 in these sentences:

1. __比女人高嗎？
2. __不能沒有事做。
3. __都會死。

Exercise 76

Supply 認識 or 知道 in the following:

1. 你__我的名字嗎？
2. 我不__你今天要來。
3. 你是怎麼__她的？
4. 要是我看見那個字，我一定__。
5. 你__回家的路不__？

Exercise 77
(Resultative Verb Compounds)

Translate the following into Chinese:

1. He broke a mirror.
2. Can you see that bird in the tree?
3. She can't understand what I'm saying.
4. I managed to borrow that book.
5. Can you smell it?
6. I'll be able to find you wherever you go.
7. I must learn to master Chinese.
8. Is she asleep?

Exercise 78 (上算)

Translate the following into Chinese:

1. It's a real bargain.
2. It's cheaper to buy on the streets.

Exercise 79 (是……的)

Translate the following into Chinese:

1. I came from England.
2. He came yesterday.
3. It cost me one hundred dollars.
4. How did you fix it?
5. We came by car.

Exercise 80 (是……的 and 了)

Translate the following into Chinese:

1. I paid three hundred dollars for that watch.
2. When did you start to learn Chinese?
3. How long have you been working for him?
4. Where did you grow up?
5. Who bought this car for you?
6. I bought a car.
7. How did he fix the radio?
8. Did they get married four years ago?
9. Have you started to write characters yet?
10. He has fixed your car already. (Use — construction)

Exercise 81 (試試，想要)

Translate the following into Chinese:

1. Have you tried this hotel?
2. You dare hit me? Try it!
3. He tried to help me.
4. Who are you trying to kid?
5. Try it. It's delicious!

Exercise 82

Use 收 or 收到 in the following:

1. 今天是星期天，不__信。
2. 昨天他__了一封電報。
3. 你把衣服__進來了嗎？
4. 那本字典你__了沒有？
5. __禮物是不可以的。
6. 我只管__錢，別的不管。

Exercise 83

Use 摔 or 掉 in the following:

1. 他不小心__在地上了。
2. 鐘從牆上__下來了。
3. 葉子從樹上__下來了。
4. 別把玻璃杯__了。
5. 你__着了吧？疼不疼？
6. 誰的錢包__在地上了？
7. 飛機__下來了，可是他没__死。

Exercise 84

Use 睡覺 or 睡着 in the following:

1. 他總是一__了就睡得很熟。
2. 我累的時候，一躺下就能__。
3. 有的人__要半天才能__。
4. 你有__午__的習慣嗎？

Exercise 85

Use 送 or 帶 in the following:

1. 天晚了，我__你回宿舍吧。
2. 誰認識路誰__路。
3. 不必__了。請回，請回。
4. 請你__孩子到外頭去玩兒去。
5. 別忘了__你男朋友給我們看看。
6. 每天早上我都__孩子去上學。

Exercise 86

Supply 算，算了，算上，算出來 or 算完 in these sentences:

1. 請你__我們一個月的生活費是多少。
2. 這道題他__了半天都没__。
3. __吧，明天再談。
4. __今天，已經過了兩個星期了。
5. 你們一起__這道題，看看誰先__。
6. 請__賬吧。
7. 別把我__。
8. 要是你不會開車就__。

Exercise 87
(Verb-Object Compounds)

Translate the following into Chinese:

1. Do you drive?
2. How often do you go shopping?
3. My daughter doesn't like to write.
4. Some people say the Cantonese eat five times a day.
5. I write to my family once a week.
6. Do you study at night too?
7. He loves to drink.
8. Don't fight!

Exercise 88

Supply 爲，給 or 替 in the following:

1. 你__我用了多少錢？
2. __了買這件衣服，我去過了很多商店。
3. 我__你把功課做好了。
4. 他們__我們介紹了本地的情況。
5. 人人__我，我__人人。
6. 老師__我們講了一個故事。
7. 生日那天，媽媽__我買了一隻錶。
8. 誰能__她去取行李？

Exercise 89

Supply 想起來 or 想出來 in these sentences:

1. 我__他是誰了。
2. 你__得__我們是哪年認識的嗎？
3. 他最近__一種新式電話機。
4. 她一__考試__就怕。
5. 我__不__她爲甚麼生我的氣。
6. 我__不__小偷是怎麼進屋子的。

Exercise 90 (些)

Translate the following into Chinese:

1. Are you any better?
2. I want to do some shopping.
3. The weather is getting better.
4. Put those books on the table.

Exercise 91

Supply 學 or 學會 in the following:

1. 我已經__怎麼用電腦了。
2. 要__一樣東西，就得把它__，把它學好。
3. 他__騎自行車，__了一個月還沒__。

Exercise 92 (要)

Translate the following into Chinese:

1. She's going to send me a book.
2. We're going to France tomorrow.
3. Don't fight!
4. You should eat more vegetables, and less meat.
5. They want to move to the countryside.
6. You should be a little more careful next time.

Exercise 93 (要是……就)

Translate the following into Chinese:

1. I wouldn't buy it if I didn't have to.
2. They would have met me if they had gone there.
3. If I were you, I wouldn't promise him anything.
4. If I'm mistaken, you're mistaken, too.
5. I think it would be much better if you got a job.

Exercise 94 (一……就)

Translate the following into Chinese:

1. She left as soon as she had finished her coffee.
2. I'll write you as soon as I get there.
3. He'll watch TV as soon as his classes are over.
4. As soon as he entered, everybody clapped their hands to welcome him.
5. Whenever she has money, she'll buy books.

Exercise 95 (一……也/都)

Translate the following into Chinese:

1. She didn't say a word today.
2. I haven't had *Longjing* tea once.
3. He was so nervous that he couldn't even write a single character.
4. He doesn't drink at all.
5. There was nothing to worry about at all.

Exercise 96 (一點兒)

Translate the following into Chinese:

1. There is only a little time left.
2. I understand a little of what he says.
3. Give me a little of that wine, please.
4. She knows a little of everything.
5. Can you drive a little faster?
6. Have some more (food).

Exercise 97

Use 一定 or 一定得 in these sentences:

1. 你__不喜歡去。
2. 你__幫我忙。
3. 你__不要告訴她。
4. 你__等我半天了。
5. 你今天__把信寫好。

Exercise 98

Use 以前 or 以後 in the following:

1. __她是小姐，一年__她就是張太太了。
2. 買鞋__，當然得先試試。

3. 我大學畢業___可能出國學習。
4. 一個月___，我就要當爸爸了。
5. 他是我___的老闆，現在已經退休了。
6. ___吃飯別等我。

Exercise 99

Use 用功 or 努力 in these sentences:

1. 爲世界和平而___！
2. 工人從早到晚___地工作。
3. 學習漢字，不___不行。
4. 別太___讀書，也要注意身體。

Exercise 100 ([一]些 and 有的)

Translate the following into Chinese:

1. They need some medicine.
2. She has some jewelery, but not enough.
3. Some people like Guilin's mountains, others prefer its waters.
4. Some new books are very helpful to students of Chinese.
5. We have dumplings for dinner at times.
6. Have some more fruit.

Exercise 101

Use 又 or 再 in these sentences:

1. 他___來借錢來了。
2. 飛機___發生意外了。
3. 下次來，別___買東西了。
4. 湯不夠鹹，___放點兒鹽。
5. 請___唱一個。
6. 她___唱了一個歌。
7. 他吃了一碗飯，___吃了一碗。
8. 他會開飛機，___會修理飛機。
9. ___來一碗飯，好嗎？
10. ___冷的天我們也去游泳。

Exercise 102 (有點兒)

Translate the following into Chinese:

1. I'm a little afraid of you.
2. She feels a bit homesick.
3. He's somewhat unwilling to go.
4. I feel somewhat embarrassed at seeing her.
5. The boy is somewhat like a grown-up now.

Exercise 103

Use 有意思 or 感 (有)興趣 in these sentences:

1. 我對中國字很___。
2. 這是一本___的兒童故事書。
3. 當音樂老師___嗎？
4. 她對音樂非常___。
5. 跟這位老人談話真___。

Exercise 104 (在 after Verbs)

Translate the following into Chinese:

1. She lives on the west coast by the seaside.
2. I grew up in Beijing.
3. Put your hands on your head.
4. Would you stand between those two buildings?
5. Write your name in the top right corner, please.
6. He bumped his head against the door.
7. Please sit over here.
8. Don't stand in front of the TV.

Exercise 105

Use 早上 or 上午 in these sentences:

1. 你___幾點上班。
2. 我___在家，下午去看病。
3. 我___一起來就看報。
4. 你有一個___可以唸書。

Exercise 106

Use 長 or 長得 in the following:

1. 這個青年人__真結實。
2. 蘋果樹又__高了。
3. 這匹馬__又高又壯。
4. 你__白頭髮了嗎？
5. 孩子都__大了。
6. 他的鼻子__真高。

Exercise 107（着涼，傷風，感冒，發燒）

Translate the following into Chinese:

1. She has a high fever.
2. I caught a cold last night.
3. It's easy to catch a cold in this kind of weather.
4. The boy has a touch of fever.

Exercise 108
(Verb + 着 and 在 + Verb)

Translate the following into Chinese:

1. The front door is locked.
2. What are you cooking?
3. I drink while watching TV.
4. The Chinese team is practising volleyball.
5. She's lying in bed.
6. While walking down the street, he suddenly fell down.
7. Is she typing a letter?
8. He's singing aloud on the sofa.

Exercise 109（這，那）

Translate the following into Chinese:

1. That's the way to do it.
2. That's not very funny.
3. Who's that?
4. That's that.
5. The man over there is my friend.

Exercise 110

Use 值錢 or 值得 in these sentences:

1. 這個電影__看。
2. 這件事不__提。
3. 這張畫很__。
4. 我没有甚麼__的東西可以賣。
5. 黃山__去看嗎？
6. 買這件棉衣用了一百塊錢，__嗎？

Exercise 111（重 and 厚）

Translate the following into Chinese:

1. This blanket is rather heavy.
2. She has a heavy French accent.
3. He wears a heavy coat.
4. The luggage is too heavy for one person to carry.
5. This dictionary is thick and heavy.

Exercise 112（字 and 句）

Translate the following into Chinese:

1. She didn't say a word.
2. He is a man of many words.
3. Don't speak empty words to me.
4. I'd like to say a few words on this subject.
5. She writes beautifully.
6. Do you recognize this character?

Exercise 113

Use 走，走走，走路 or 走着 in these sentences:

1. __去太慢，還是坐車去好。
2. 咱們出去__，好嗎？
3. 他是哪天__的？
4. 飯後__對身體好。
5. 他__ __突然笑了起來。
6. 勞駕，去郵局怎麼__？
7. 鐘又不__了。

Exercise 114

Use 走，去 or 離開 in these sentences:

1. 我們幾點鐘__？
2. 你是哪年__台灣的？
3. 她是哪年__的？
4. 我們__着__嗎？

Key to Exercises

Exercise 1

1．吧　2．呢　3．吧　4．嗎　5．呢
6．嗎　7. 呢　8. 吧

Exercise 2

1. 她把我昨天買的糖吃了。
2. 我把錢找給他了。
3. 孩子把手洗得乾淨極了。
4. 你一定要把中文學好。
5. 回家後把歌兒練練。
6. 你千萬別把這件事告訴她。

Exercise 3

1. 半　2. 一半　3. 半，一半
4. 一半，一半　5. 一個半

Exercise 4

1. 幫　2. 幫　3. 幫忙　4. 幫忙
5. 幫忙

Exercise 5

1. three times　2. twice　3. three times　4. two and a half times

Exercise 6

1. 我比妹妹高多了。
2. 他比爸爸小 20 歲。
3. 德國車比日本車貴得多。
4. 弟弟比我矮一點兒。

Exercise 7

1. 你甚麼時候中學畢業？
2. 大學畢業後，他就上研究院了。

Exercise 8

1. 請別客氣。
2. 謝謝你的幫助。別客氣。
3. 別客氣，我不渴。

Exercise 9

1. 另外　2. 另外　3. 別的　4. 別的
5. 另外

Exercise 10

1. 不　2. 別　3. 不　4. 別　5. 不

Exercise 11

1. 我想她不來了。
2. 我們不覺得/不認爲那樣對。
3. 我今天不想出去。
4. 你不認爲快下雨了嗎？
5. 她不想家。

Exercise 12

1. 你才是小偷呢。
2. 他才坐下。
3. 我學中文才學了一個月。

Exercise 13

1. 長　2. 久　3. 長/久　4. 久

Exercise 14

1. 吃不下　2. 吃得了　3. 吃得到
4. 吃得着　5. 吃得了

Exercise 15

1. 出過事　2. 意外　3. 出，事
4. 出事　5. 意外

Exercise 16

1. 從來不　2. 從來沒　3. 一直沒
4. 從來不，一直沒

Exercise 17

1. 大家　2. 大家　3. 每個人　4. 大家
5. 大家，大家　6. 每個人

Exercise 18

1. 拿　2. 帶　3. 拿　4. 帶　5. 帶
6. 帶

Exercise 19

1. 不美　2. 聰明　3. 厲害　4. 不貴
5. 慢

Exercise 20

1. 他昨天收到了一個包裹。
2. 你看到哪兒了？
3. 你聽到那個消息了嗎？
4. 我昨天想到你了。
5. 你聞到了嗎？
6. 你們談到第三點了嗎？

Exercise 21

1. –,–　2. +,+　3. +　4. –,–
5. +,+,+　6. +

Exercise 22

1. 約　2. 定約會　3. 掛號　4. 約
5. 掛號　6. 約會

Exercise 23

1. 東西　2. 事情　3. 事情　4. 東西
5. 東西

Exercise 24

1. 男孩子都要聽你講故事。
2. 你們都來了嗎？
3. 把你知道的都告訴我們。
4. 我哪兒都找過他了。
5. 都做完了。
6. 她的臉都紅了。

Exercise 25

1. 勞駕　2. 對不起　3. 請問　4. 勞駕
5. 對不起

Exercise 26

1. 跟　2. 跟　3. 對　4. 對　5. 對

Exercise 27

1. 他多買了一個帽子。
2. 請多多指教。
3. 我們希望多看看這個城。
4. 我教書教了二十多年了。
5. 越多越好。

Exercise 28

1. 兩，二　2. 兩　3. 二/兩　4. 兩

Exercise 29

1. 菜　2. 米，飯　3. 菜　4. 米飯
5. 菜，飯

Exercise 30

1. 假期　2. 放假　3. 放假　4. 假期
5. 假，放

Exercise 31

1. 順便　2. 順便　3. 方便　4. 方便
5. 方便

Exercise 32

1. 剛　2. 剛才　3. 剛　4. 剛才/剛
5. 剛剛

Exercise 33

1. 他買給她一隻手錶。
2. 你可以借給我三百塊嗎？
3. 她要送給我一些新郵票。
4. 我把汽車賣給他了。
5. 你把信交給誰了？

Exercise 34

1. 跟　2. 也　3. 跟　4. 也　5. 也
6. 也

Exercise 35

1. 我們的時間夠不夠？
2. 飯還不夠熟。
3. 夠了！
4. 東西不夠六個人吃。
5. 那兒的情形夠嚴重的。

Exercise 36

1. 對於　2. 關於　3. 對於　4. 關於
5. 關於

Exercise 37

1. 你開過車嗎？
2. 你愛上過人嗎？
3. 買過東西我們就回家。

Exercise 38

1. 還是　2. 還是/或者　3. 還是/或是
4. 還是

Exercise 39

1. 她很會做菜。
2. 他們會結婚嗎？
3. 你會説廣東話嗎？
4. 我不會開車。

Exercise 40

1. 他哪兒都沒去。
2. 我今天誰都不要見。
3. 她甚麼都沒説。
4. 我甚麼魚都喜歡吃。
5. 她説她哪兒都要去看看。
6. 誰都有自己的問題。
7. 我今天晚上哪兒都不去。

Exercise 41

1. 家　2. 家家　3. 房子　4. 房子/家

Exercise 42

1. 她昨天借了一個收音機。
2. 甚麼都別借給他。
3. 他們甚麼都沒跟我們借。
4. 我可以借你的手提包嗎？

Exercise 43

1. 接　2. 接　3. 接到　4. 接
5. 接到

Exercise 44

1. 記得　2. 記，得　3. 記住　4. 記得
5. 記得住

Exercise 45

1. 我就有一個朋友。
2. 他們就到了。
3. 我們下午四點就下班。
4. 我吃完晚飯就來。

Exercise 46

1. 才 2. 就 3. 才，就 4. 就
5. 才 6. 才

Exercise 47

1. 看 2. 看 3. 看，看見 4. 見(見)
5. 看見 6. 見見 7. 看 8. 看

Exercise 48

1. 班 2. 課 3. 課 4. 班 5. 班

Exercise 49

1. 可憐 2. 可憐 3. 可惜 4. 可惜
5. 可惜

Exercise 50

1. 你可坐下。
2. 你可以開我的車。
3. 你可以坐船到上海去嗎？
4. 在這不可以抽煙。

Exercise 51

1. 怕 2. 恐怕 3. 怕 4. 恐怕
5. 怕

Exercise 52

1. 他們不來了。
2. 她越來越漂亮了。
3. 我做了很多年了。
4. 太好了！
5. 昨天我到那個飯館去了。

Exercise 53

1. 過 2. 過 3. 了 4. 了
5. 了，了 6. 了 7. 過，了 8. 過
9. 過 10. 了

Exercise 54

1. 從 2. 離 3. 離 4. 從 5. 離
6. 從，從

Exercise 55

1. 離不開 2. 離得開 3. 走得開
4. 走得開 5. 離得開

Exercise 56

1. 他連做菜都不會。
2. 她連法文也會說。
3. 我連他的姓都忘了。
4. 他連他太太也不聽。
5. 可憐蟲！你連一毛錢都沒有？

Exercise 57

1. 忙甚麼 2. 別忙 3. 別忙 4. 不忙
5. 忙甚麼 6. 不忙

Exercise 58

1. 她來不來沒關係。
2. 誰說偷東西沒關係。
3. 沒關係！我自己能做。
4. 大小都沒關係。
5. 她沒打電話沒關係。

Exercise 59

1. 他在看的書是我老師寫的。
2. 我們昨天在那個飯館吃的菜是四川菜。
3. 他買的報紙是一份英文日報。
4. 這就是我出生的地方。
5. 你最喜歡的運動是甚麼？

Exercise 60

1. 撿起來 2. 拿起 3. 拿上來
4. 拿起來 5. 撿起來

Exercise 61

1. 呢　2. 呢　3. 嗎　4. 呢　5. 呢，嗎

Exercise 62

1. 你能坐火車去嗎？
2. 你能早點兒來嗎？
3. 我能出去玩嗎？
4. 我今天不能說話。

Exercise 63

1. 會　2. 可以　3. 能　4. 可以
5. 能　6. 可以/能　7. 會　8. 會
9. 能　10. 能，能

Exercise 64

1. 1991 年 7 月 1 日星期三。
2. 今天幾號？
3. 今天星期幾？
4. 上個月是幾月？

Exercise 65

1. 看，唸　2. 唸　3. 看，唸　4. 唸/讀

Exercise 66

1. 派　2. 寄，派，寄　3. 送　4. 送
5. 派　6. 寄

Exercise 67

1. 碰　2. 碰　3. 碰到　4. 碰見/碰到/碰上　5. 碰上　6. 碰(碰)　7. 碰上
8. 碰見/碰到/碰上

Exercise 68

1. 見過面　2. 碰見　3. 見面　4. 碰見

Exercise 69

1. 輕　2. 輕　3. 薄　4. 薄，輕
5. 薄

Exercise 70

1. 請　2. 請客，請　3. 請　4. 請客
5. 請　6. 請

Exercise 71

1. 請問　2. 請　3. 請　4. 請問
5. 請　6. 請　7. 請　8. 請問

Exercise 72

1. 請　2. 叫　3. 問　4. 叫/請，問
5. 請　6. 問

Exercise 73

1. 誰……誰　2. 哪兒……哪兒
3. 誰……誰　4. 甚麼……甚麼
5. 哪……哪　6. 怎麼……怎麼
7. 甚麼……甚麼　8. 誰……誰
9. 哪兒……哪兒　10. 怎麼……怎麼

Exercise 74

1. 我們要休息休息。
2. 請你收拾收拾屋子，好嗎？
3. 他高高興興地回家了。
4. 請試試。
5. 讓我看看你的照片。
6. 先洗洗手。
7. 風輕輕地吹着。
8. 請慢慢地說。

Exercise 75

1. 男人　2. 人　3. 人

Exercise 76

1. 知道　2. 知道　3. 認識　4. 認識
5. 認識，認識

Exercise 77

1. 他打破了一面鏡子。
2. 你看得見在樹裏的那隻鳥嗎？

3. 她聽不懂我說的話。
4. 我借到那本書了。
5. 你聞得見嗎？
6. 你去哪兒我都找得到你。
7. 我一定要學會中文。
8. 她睡着了嗎？

Exercise 78

1. 真上算。
2. 在街上買上算。

Exercise 79

1. 我是從英國來的。
2. 他是昨天來的。
3. 是一百塊錢買的。
4. 你是怎麼修好的？
5. 我們是坐車來的。

Exercise 80

1. 我是用三百塊錢買的那隻手錶。
2. 你是甚麼時候開始學習中文的？
3. 你替他做事做了多久了？
4. 你是在哪兒長大的？
5. 是誰買這輛車給你的？
6. 我買了一輛汽車。
7. 他是怎麼把收音機修好的？
8. 他們是四年前結的婚嗎？
9. 你們開始學寫字了沒有？
10. 他已經把你的汽車修好了。

Exercise 81

1. 你試過這個旅館嗎？
2. 你敢打我？試試看！
3. 他想要幫我忙。
4. 你想(要)騙誰？
5. 試試，真好吃！

Exercise 82

1. 收　2. 收到　3. 收　4. 收到
5. 收　6. 收

Exercise 83

1. 摔　2. 掉　3. 掉　4. 摔　5. 摔
6. 掉　7. 摔/掉，摔

Exercise 84

1. 睡着　2. 睡着　3. 睡覺，睡着
4. 睡，覺

Exercise 85

1. 送　2. 帶　3. 送　4. 帶　5. 帶
6. 送

Exercise 86

1. 算算　2. 算，算出來　3. 算了
4. 算上　5. 算算，算出來/算完
6. 算　7. 算上　8. 算了

Exercise 87

1. 你會開車嗎？
2. 你多久買一次東西？
3. 我女兒不喜歡寫字。
4. 有人說廣東人一天吃五頓飯。
5. 我每星期寫一次信回家。
6. 你在晚上也念書嗎？
7. 他愛喝酒。
8. 別打架！

Exercise 88

1. 爲　2. 爲　3. 替　4. 給　5. 爲，爲　6. 給　7. 給　8. 替/給

Exercise 89

1. 想起來　2. 想，起來　3. 想出來
4. 想起，來　5. 想，出來　6. 想，出來

Exercise 90

1. 你好些了嗎？
2. 我要買些東西。

3. 天氣好些了。
4. 把那些書放在桌子上。

Exercise 91

1. 學會 2. 學，學會 3. 學，學，學會

Exercise 92

1. 她要寄一本書給我。
2. 我們明天要去法國。
3. 不要打架！
4. 你要多吃菜，少吃肉。
5. 他們要搬到鄉下(農村)去。
6. 你下次要小心點兒。

Exercise 93

1. 我要是不需要，就不會買。
2. 他們要是去了，就碰見我了。
3. 要是我是你，我就甚麼都不答應他。
4. 要是我錯了，你就也錯了。
5. 我想要是你有了工作就好多了。

Exercise 94

1. 她一喝完咖啡就走了。
2. 我一到那兒，就給你們寫信。
3. 他一下課就看電視。
4. 他一進去，大家就都拍手歡迎他。
5. 她一有錢就買書。

Exercise 95

1. 她今天一句話也沒說。
2. 我一次也沒喝過"龍井茶"。
3. 他緊張得一個字也寫不出來。
4. 他一點兒酒也不喝。
5. 一點也不用着急。

Exercise 96

1. 就剩下一點兒時間了。
2. 他說的話，我聽得懂一點兒。
3. 請給我一點兒那種酒。
4. 她甚麼都知道(一)點兒。
5. 你可以開快(一)點兒嗎？
6. 再吃點兒。

Exercise 97

1. 一定 2. 一定得 3. 一定 4. 一定
5. 一定得

Exercise 98

1. 以前，以後 2. 以前 3. 以後
4. 以後 5. 以前 6. 以後

Exercise 99

1. 努力 2. 努力 3. 用功/努力
4. 用功/努力

Exercise 100

1. 他們需要(一)些藥。
2. 她有些首飾，可是不夠。
3. 有的人喜歡桂林的山，有的人喜歡桂林的水。
4. 有的新書對學習漢語的學生很有幫助。
5. 有的時候，我們晚飯吃餃子。
6. 再吃(一)些水果。

Exercise 101

1. 又 2. 又 3. 再 4. 再 5. 再
6. 又 7. 又 8. 又 9. 再 10. 再

Exercise 102

1. 我有點兒怕你。
2. 她有點兒想家。
3. 他有點兒不願意去。
4. 我看見她的時候，覺得有點兒不好意思。
5. 這孩子有點兒像大人了。

Exercise 103

1. 感興趣　2. 有意思　3. 有意思
4. 感興趣　5. 有意思

Exercise 104

1. 她住在西岸靠海邊兒的地方。
2. 我長在北京。
3. 把手放在頭上。
4. 你可不可以站在那兩個大樓的中間？
5. 請把你的名字寫在右上角。
6. 他的頭碰在門上了。
7. 請坐在這邊兒。
8. 別站在電視前頭。

Exercise 105

1. 早上　2. 上午　3. 早上　4. 上午

Exercise 106

1. 長得　2. 長　3. 長得　4. 長
5. 長　6. 長得

Exercise 107

1. 她發高燒。/她發燒發得很高。
2. 我昨天晚上着涼了/着了點涼。
3. 這種天氣容易傷風/感冒/着涼。
4. 孩子有點發燒。/孩子有點兒燒。

Exercise 108

1. 前門鎖着呢。
2. 你在做甚麼菜？
3. 我喝着酒看電視。
4. 中國隊在練習排球呢。
5. 她在牀上躺着呢。
6. 他走着走着突然摔倒了。
7. 她在打信嗎？
8. 他在沙發上大聲唱着歌。

Exercise 109

1. 這樣做才對。
2. 這並不可笑。
3. 誰呀？
4. 就這樣吧。
5. 那邊那個人是我朋友。

Exercise 110

1. 值得　2. 值得　3. 值錢　4. 值錢
5. 值得　6. 值得

Exercise 111

1. 這條毯子挺厚的。
2. 她的法國口音很重。
3. 他穿着一件厚大衣。
4. 行李一個人拿太重。
5. 這本字典又厚又重。

Exercise 112

1. 她一句話也沒說。
2. 他是個話多的人。
3. 別對我說空話。
4. 關於這個題目，我願意說幾句話。
5. 她的字寫得很美。
6. 你認識這個字嗎？

Exercise 113

1. 走路　2. 走走　3. 走　4. 走路/走走
5. 走着走着　6. 走　7. 走

Exercise 114

1. 走/去/離開　2. 去/離開
3. 走/去/離開　4. 走，去

Index

(Entry numbers are given after the items)

A Guide to Proper Usage of Spoken Chinese

編著者	Tian Shou-he
發行人	魏 德 文
發行所	南天書局有限公司
地　址	台北市羅斯福路3段283巷14弄14號
電　話	(02) 2362-0190（代表號）
電　傳	(02) 2362-3834
郵　撥	01080538（南天書局帳戶）
國際書號	ISBN 957-638-347-1
版　次	一九九六年三月二版台灣一刷發行
印刷者	國順印刷有限公司
廠　址	板橋市中正路216巷2弄13號